JOHN GALBRAITH

Engineer and Educator

John Galbraith, M.A., L.L.D., 1846–1914.

PORTRAIT BY J.W.L. FORSTER

CATHERINE MORIARTY

John Galbraith
1846–1914

Engineer and Educator
A Portrait

Faculty of Applied Science and Engineering
University of Toronto

© Catherine Moriarty 1989
Printed in Canada by University of Toronto Press

Canadian Cataloguing in Publication Data

Moriarty, Catherine B. (Catherine Beatrix), 1920–
John Galbraith, 1846–1914: engineer and
educator

Includes bibliographical references.
ISBN 0-7727-6700-9

1. Galbraith, John, 1846–1914. 2. Engineers –
Canada – Biography. 3. College teachers – Ontario –
Toronto – Biography. 4. College administrators –
Ontario – Toronto – Biography. 5. Engineering –
Study and teaching – Canada – History.
6. University of Toronto. Faculty of Applied
Science and Engineering – History. I. University of
Toronto. Faculty of Applied Science and Engineering.
II. Title.

TA140.G44M67 1989   620'.0092'4   C89-093565-3

Published with the aid of a grant from the
Faculty of Applied Science and Engineering
University of Toronto

CONTENTS

Foreword   vii
Introduction   ix

1 Child of the Steam Age   1
2 Student, Engineer, Teacher   9
3 Professor – "for the love of it"   18
4 Northern Adventure   28
5 Family Life   41
6 Varsity in the 1890s   45
7 Northern Summers   50
8 A New Era   58
9 Dean and Commissioner   67
10 Toronto and Go Home Bay   77
11 Conserving Canada's Resources   81
12 Full Circle   88
13 The Beauty of the Evening   96

Appendix   105
A Note on Sources   122

FOREWORD

JOHN GALBRAITH was a visionary who believed that engineers should be educated widely in technical subjects and in the humanities. His drive to replace the apprenticeship training of the day with a formal university education in engineering was realized at the University of Toronto, where he laid the foundations for engineering education in Canada.

Dean Galbraith encouraged his students to inquire and analyze, to have historical consciousness, and to learn about other cultures and the arts. His model of the ideal engineering education is even more valid today, and we must strive to achieve it.

As an example to the young people embarking on their engineering education, Professor Galbraith had all the qualities he espoused. He was an explorer of the intellectual and the physical world and a linguist who spoke thirteen languages, including several Indian dialects. He was also known as a man with a strong social conscience, which led to his participation in the Royal Commission on the Quebec Bridge collapse and in philanthropic work.

Catherine Moriarty, Dean Galbraith's granddaughter, has given us a comprehensive portrait that offers insights into the man, the engineering school at the University of Toronto, and the times. The Faculty of Applied Science and Engineering, its friends, and its alumni have gained an invaluable account of a most illustrious engineer.

Gary W. Heinke
Dean, Faculty of Applied Science and Engineering

INTRODUCTION

I NEVER KNEW my grandfather in person for he died before any of his grandchildren were born. I did know him through my mother, who loved to tell us about her childhood. Grandfather's picture had a place of honour in our dining room and I spent many hours reading, curled up in his favourite leather rocking chair. As I grew older I became aware that he was not only special to his family but also to the engineering profession of our country and was admired as a great Canadian.

I started to write his story for my children and grandchildren using articles, letters and scrapbooks that my mother kept and material my cousins lent me. While visiting in Toronto I talked to old friends of the family and went to the University of Toronto Archives where I met Harold Averill, Archivist. It was he who first suggested I write a biography for publication. He provided me with all of the research material available in the Archives and in turn I took my original documents to him for safe-keeping. He made arrangements for me to meet Professor M.N. Huggins, B.A.Sc., M.A.Sc. of the Faculty of Applied Science and Engineering, University of Toronto. Professor Huggins admired John Galbraith and was interested in the idea of a biography. It was he who introduced to me to Professor Ian Dalton, B.A.Sc., M.S.

I could never have done this book without Professor Dalton. After the death of Professor Huggins he spent countless hours answering my questions, reading and critizing early drafts and suggesting improvements. He introduced me to Dean G.R. Slemon, B.A.Sc., M.A.Sc., D.I.C., Ph.D.,D.Sc. who encouraged my effort and the present Dean G.W. Heinke, B.A.Sc., M.A.Sc., Ph.D. who made a dream a reality.

Professor Dalton has continued to act as the link between me and all of the others involved in publication.

I also want to thank my editor, John Parry, who tactfully helped to smooth the rough edges.

Lastly, this book could never have been written without the continued help and interest of my late husband, Dr. Edmund Joseph Moriarty, who unfailingly supported my enthusiasm.

JOHN GALBRAITH

Engineer and Educator

CHAPTER ONE

Child of the Steam Age

THE SCHOOL OF PRACTICAL SCIENCE in Toronto celebrated its fiftieth anniversary in 1927. To mark this occasion, a bronze bust of John Galbraith, often referred to as the "founder of engineering in Canada," was presented to the School by his former students. The Rev. Canon Cody, Chairman of the Board of Governors of the University of Toronto, accepted the likeness on behalf of the University and spoke of John Galbraith:

He was wise in judgement, equable in temper, and lovable in character and carried the school from strength to strength. He was a great man, a great leader, a great teacher, and one of the builders of Canada. Men trained by him have had an extensive and leading part in building the railways and developing the waterpower, industries and other resources of the country.

He was steadfast in purpose, of wonderful integrity, and possessed of a great humanity, and this memorial to him is but a fraction of the monument to him which is the love and admiration of thousands of his former students.

John Anderson Galbraith was the first Professor of Engineering of the School of Practical Science, was its first Principal, and became the first Dean of Applied Science and Engineering when the School affiliated with the University of Toronto in 1906 and held that position until his death in 1914.

He was born in Montreal, Canada East, on September 5, 1846, at the beginning of an exciting period in Canada's history. The vast mineral and natural resources were in the process of development, roads were being laid out and bridges built, and trains were beginning to rumble across newly laid tracks.

His father, Thomas Galbraith, born in 1822, in Coldstream, Berwickshire, on the banks of the Tweed in Scotland, had emigrated to Canada in 1834, settling in Montreal. At nineteen he was an accountant with Henry Morgan, a good friend, who started the first Morgan's department store in Montreal. Morgan acted as groomsman at Thomas's wedding on November 26, 1844. The bride, Jane Anderson, was the daughter of John Anderson of Eskdalemuir, Dumfriesshire, who had also emigrated to Montreal and married a French Canadian, Jane LeBeau. The young Galbraiths settled down to raise a family. Their first son was stillborn in 1845. During the next five years they became the proud parents of three sons, John, born on September 5, 1846, William, in 1848, and Thomas, in 1849, and a daughter Jean, in 1851.

When Jean was still an infant the family moved to Port Hope, Canada West, where Thomas went into partnership with his brother-in-law, William Anderson, in a drygoods store. To move a family several hundred miles in the early 1850s was not easy. Travellers had two options: steamer or stage-coach. It took several days to make the trip over rough roads by stage-coach.

Port Hope was a small town on the shores of Lake Ontario, approximately 70 miles east of Toronto. Its history went back to the seventeenth century, when the Sulpician Fathers ministered to the Mississaugua Indians of the area, who fished and hunted in the creeks and woods and lived in a village called Gochingomink. In 1778 Peter Smith, a fur trader, moved in and built a log cabin. He was an honest man and a good hunter, and before long he gained the respect of all who knew him. His trading post became known as Smith's Creek. Settlers arrived. Indians and whites lived together in harmony, although difficulties arose over flour. The closest grist mills were in Belleville and Kingston. Grain had to be transported, by water in summer or overland by sled in winter. In 1797 the government of Upper Canada offered another Smith (Elias) and Jonathan Walton a Crown Patent of 200 acres each, on condition that they each build a grist mill and bring in forty settlers apiece

2

from the United States. The first Post Office was opened in 1817 under the name of Smith's Creek; however, the town eventually became known as Toronto in legal documents. At a public meeting in 1819 the name Port Hope was accepted. In 1834, on March 6, an Act of Parliament incorporated Port Hope as a town.

By the time the Galbraith family moved there in 1852, Port Hope had grown into a thriving, dynamic centre. Thomas built a large home on the outskirts of town, where three more sons were added to the family, James in 1853, and twins in 1858. James died two days after his third birthday and one of the twins, a boy, four days after birth. The other, Robert Alfred, never robust, died in his teens. In the 1860s the family moved to Ridout Street, into a smaller place known as Forge Cottage, and there Thomas paid rent for the rest of his life. Jane used to tell one of her daughters-in-law that they could have bought it over and over again for what they paid out in rent. It was a charming Georgian cottage, set back from the street on a wide lawn, among maple and oak trees. It was built of soft, red Port Hope brick and featured an eyebrow window over the front door. The floors throughout were pine. There was one fireplace, a dug-out basement, and one of the best sweet-water brick wells in town. The cottage, situated on three lots, had purposely been built only one and a half stories high by Thomas Spry, a blacksmith, in 1850, in order to lessen property taxes, which were extremely high. "I do like my old house," Jane wrote her granddaughter in 1904. "I am writing in the dining room and have a good fire in the stove. It is very comfortable, but my thoughts go back to the time when my table was surrounded by readers. I think the happiest time of my life was when my children were all around me studying their lessons, and then, afterward, reading some interesting book."

Thomas remained in drygoods for only eight years before going to work for a Port Hope newspaper, the *Guide*. For a time he was publisher of the Port Hope paper the *Valuator*. By the late 1870's he was living alone in Montreal where he was the Canadian Agent for an Old Country paper, the *Scottish American Journal*. In later years he, along with his son, Tom, published the first financial paper on Wall Street.

Jane Galbraith stayed at home in Port Hope caring for their children. Jane also wrote editorials for the Guide. Years later her daughter-in-law May (William's wife) wrote to her niece: "Both she and her husband had more ability than their three daughters-in-law put together, but never in a word or a look did those clever people let us know it."

Although Thomas was rarely at home, he was a concerned father and wrote to his family every day. He and his wife passed on to their children the Scottish attributes of thrift and industry, along with a strong Presbyterian faith. In Port Hope the family joined the First Presbyterian Church, where Jane took an active part in all forms of church work. When the Port Hope branch of the *Woman's Foreign Missionary Society* of the First Presbyterian Church was formed, she was appointed Secretary, afterward Vice-president; a short time later she was elected a life member. The *Guide*, described her as a "woman of vigorous mind, of a literary turn, and of excellent judgement."

The family was not well off, and its home was not large. The parlour was comfortably cluttered, music books were always open on the piano, and formal family pictures in ornate gilded frames graced the tables and hung on the walls. Everywhere there were books, in Greek, Latin, and French, as well as the great English classics in prose and poetry. A Bible rested in a place of honour, along with a well-worn volume of John Bunyan's *Pilgrim's Progress*, with a white satin ribbon marking the current page.

Sundays in the Galbraith home were invariably the same. They never owned a horse and carriage, and so they walked to church. After dinner at noon, they read a passage from the Bible or *Pilgrim's Progress* and wrote letters. Not only music but studying and reading were permitted, but on no account were the children to desecrate the Sabbath by running and playing out of doors.

Jane Galbraith was not a beautiful woman. She had a narrow face, with a wide forehead, and her full cheeks made her face appear rounder than it actually was. Hazel eyes with dark eyebrows dominated it, and her long nose and ears were prominent. Her usually severe expression was softened by the kindness in her eyes. She wore her dark hair parted in the middle, drawn back, braided, and wound at the back of her head, according to the custom of the day. She was short, but an erect carriage added height and dignity to her small frame. Her husband and her sons were not tall; John, the eldest, was the shortest of them all. He also had a slight stutter and hesitancy of speech which remained with him all of his life.

Weekday evenings, the family sat around the long pine table in the kitchen under the hanging china lamp. Jane wrote daily to her husband. They all enjoyed the letters he sent from his boarding-house in New York or Montreal, sometimes in English, sometimes in French, and always describing everyday happenings in detail. The children studied their lessons while their mother did her mending. The evening ended with one of them reading aloud from some favourite classic.

While life at home was quiet and orderly, the town bustled with activity. Because Port Hope was on Lake Ontario, it had had a busy harbour since early days, particularly for the lumber trade. About the time that the family moved there, a Harbour Commission had been formed and the former haphazard collection of wharfs and piers transformed into a safe harbour. With the introduction of daily steamship service from 1840 on and the railway in 1856 the town flourished. Young John enjoyed all the activity that he saw around him. Horses and carriages regularly passed by his home, heading down the hill toward the centre of town and the harbour. Most of the early buildings were made of wood; consequently fire was a hazard. It was common to see boys running after the volunteers as they answered the call of the large fire bell. Other men urged on the team of horses that pulled the pump wagon, but the volunteers were no match for a fire. For many years the charred wood of old buildings stood in sharp contrast to the modern brick of the new. Nearer the water the strong odour of new leather from the tannery mixed with the woodsy smell of sawdust flying from the saws at the mill. A large woollen mill stood close by Smith Creek, and after school small boys spent hours playing on its banks, fishing and catching tadpoles.

Nearby trains rumbled over new track. In the machine shops, anvils rang loudly and sparks flew as iron met iron. John watched fascinated as the men worked on new railway stock or repaired the huge engines. Helm's foundry was another of his after-school haunts, and there he observed the care that the men took as they forged gears and other machinery parts.

Another favourite spot of his was the harbour. It was a busy place, because rivers and lakes were the most common means of transportation. Sailing ships travelled between Toronto and Montreal, and three-masted schooners were a common sight. Groups of passengers waited patiently by their bags and bundles for steamships to take them to other ports along the lake. Breezes rippled the long skirts of the women, whose large hats perched precariously on their heads, fastened with long hatpins. Prim little girls were dressed in long dresses and coats like their mothers, their hats firmly tied on with ribbons; high-button boots completed their outfits. Excited small boys ran up and down the docks – in short pants if the weather was fine, in breeches when it was cold. The shouts of men mingled with the shrill, harsh cries of seagulls, which swooped into the lake, greedy for scraps of food. At one dock, men loaded lumber onto ships; at another, they unloaded coal. Wooden boxes of Port Hope alcohol, a product of one of its distilleries, were shipped to Montreal to be turned into gin, rum, or brandy and then returned as an import.

Deep down on the bottom of the harbour, the shadowy hulk of the schooner *Niagara* was still visible. She was driven ashore one bitter night in early December 1856 while bringing coal from Bond Head to Port Hope. By the light of lanterns the townspeople gathered to watch the rescue. The captain and his five crew men were hanging on to the rigging to escape the angry waves. One rescuer with a five-man crew started out but failed to reach the wreck. Then another boat went out and swamped as it reached the wreck; its captain and one of his men drowned. Then the first boat went out again and rescued all the men, to the cheers of the onlookers.

That same year the first train travelled to Port Hope from Toronto. The whole town turned out to see it, and the station was decorated with bunting and flags. The passengers were dressed in their best clothes, the whistles blew, and the town band played. Six weeks later, on October 14, the Albert Viaduct opened to carry the train over swampy ground on the eastern edge of town toward Montreal. A month later, when the first train of the Grand Trunk

6

line made a short stop in Port Hope, on its first journey from Toronto to Montreal, only school boys were there to watch and cheer. By the time John was in his teens, the trains were commonplace.

Every weekday at noon, steam whistles in the factories blew, and the whole town stopped working. Men poured out of the railway yards, the woollen mills, the tannery, and the small shops to walk home for their main meal of the day.

This then, was John Galbraith's home town, an active, vigorous, dynamic centre, yet small enough that he had the freedom to wander at will, observing and learning about a variety of industries and close to the woods and the water he loved.

John received his early education at the Port Hope Grammar School in the late 1850s. There he was fortunate to come under the influence of John Gordon, a man educated in Britain and a dedicated teacher. It did not take Gordon long to recognize the extraordinary ability of his young student, and he took extra pains to challenge John's intellect and curiousity. One of his early concerns was that his young student was too intense and serious. However, he soon discovered that John was able to defend himself in the school yard and was popular with his peers. By the time John finished his schooling in 1862, at the age of seventeen, the book shelves in his home overflowed with his prizes. Not only did he do well in Mathematics, but he stood first in Latin, French, Greek, and, in fact, every subject he tackled.

The other man to have a great influence in John's life at that time was George Stewart, a surveyor, a tall, handsome man, with powerful shoulders. He also recognized the potential of his young friend and often took him out in the woods on a Saturday afternoon. He gave the boy his first lessons in the ways of the wild. Stewart had the respect and admiration of the Indians in the area for his knowledge of wildlife and woodlore, and he passed on much of what he had learned to John. It was Stewart who showed him how to do a survey, explaining the necessity of accuracy in planning a bridge or laying out a road. It was he who gave John his first copy of Rankine's *Civil Engineering*, a book that Galbraith prized all his life. But George Stewart was more than a competent surveyor and

7

woodsman; he was also a scholar and demonstrated the value of a well-rounded, classical education to his young protégé. From him young John Galbraith got both his determination to become an engineer and his lifelong love of the wilderness.

CHAPTER TWO

Student, Engineer, Teacher

YOUNG JOHN GALBRAITH fully intended to go to McGill University in Montreal when he finished his schooling, to fulfil his dream of becoming an engineer. His father lived there a good part of the time, and there were relatives there on both sides of his family. Unfortunately, when he made inquiries in 1862, he discovered that the only engineering course offered had been withdrawn. The alternative was the University of Toronto.

In 1798 Lieutenant-Governor John Graves Simcoe had promoted the idea of a university in Upper Canada, but it was not until he left office in 1799 that the Legislative Assembly petitioned the British Parliament to endow one. A Royal Charter was granted in 1827, and in 1828 the Government set aside 225,944 acres of Crown Reserves to endow the University of King's College. It was another fifteen years before lectures began. King's College was founded under the auspices of the Church of England, with the proviso that the faculty members belong to that denomination and also that all students conform to certain religious criteria. Understandably, this caused considerable problems, and in 1849 the Parliament of the Province of Canada secularized King's College. Another allotment of Crown Lands was added, and a new Charter granted, under the name University of Toronto. Using the University of London (England) as a model, the Province made important changes in 1853. The University was to be governed by a Senate, some of whose members were elected by the Provincial Government. It was to be merely a degree-conferring and examination body, and all its teaching functions were to be transferred to the newly formed University College.

This was the arrangement when John Galbraith arrived in Toronto to apply for engineering in the early-1860s. He was bitterly disappointed to discover that a course offered at University College was not adequate and did not lead to a degree. Engineering was considered at the time a mere trade. The usual method of training was for an aspiring engineer to apprentice himself to a practising engineer for a time, then present himself to the university to write an examination and, if successful, receive a diploma.

While undecided as to his next step, John was introduced to John Cherriman, Professor of Mathematics, Physics and Natural Philosophy. John told him of his intentions and also of his great disappointment. The Professor invited John into his office and questioned him about his schooling in Port Hope, his recreational interests, and particularly his friendship with the engineer and surveyor George Stewart. Cherriman suggested that even if the University did not offer formal engineering courses, many other offerings were of great value to an engineer. As a consequence, John enrolled in Arts, with Mathematics as a major, and in Modern Languages and Natural Sciences. Again he had encountered an outstanding teacher, who would influence his future. John Cherriman was a fellow of St. John's College, Cambridge and finished sixth in the Mathematical Tripos there when Lord Kelvin was second wrangler.

Thus John settled in to study and take part in university life. He moved into a boarding-house on Czar Street, close by the University. The homes on the street had been virtually taken over by the University to provide living quarters for out-of-town students. There was also a residence at University College, but this was not large. Besides his studies, John took an active part in student athletic life and joined the University Rifles. Many small towns in Ontario had voluntary military companies, and the University of Toronto was no exception. During the summer months, John returned to Port Hope to work as an apprentice surveyor under his old friend George Stewart.

In June 1866, John was working on the Foley Township Survey with George Stewart, near Parry Sound, laying out concession roads. On June 12 the Indian guides returned to the campsite from Parry Sound, bringing newspapers telling of trouble at Ridgeway, Ontario, on June 2. According to the report, a group of 800 Fenians had crossed Lake Erie, encamped at Ridgeway, and attacked a group of volunteers. The Fenians were the US branch of the Irish Revolutionary Brotherhood, founded in Dublin in 1858. They had already caused numerous problems in the United States, and now some members urged an invasion of Canada. Their plan was to use this country as a base from which to invade Ireland and force out the British. An attack on Canada would at the very least focus British attention.

John was very upset when he read about the attack in the paper. His regiment, the University Rifles, had been involved in the fighting, and the article named two of his close friends, who were among the ten killed. In his diary he stated that he did not sleep at all well that night and felt miserable all day. That evening Stewart gave him permission to join his regiment, but it was a week before he was able to get away because of a surveying error, which had to be corrected before he was free to go.

He left one evening after dinner for Parry Sound, where he slept in a proper bed for the first time in three months. At 6 a.m. he took the steamer for Collingwood, arriving twelve hours later. There he met three companies – two rifles and one infantry – on their way home from the front. He also read in the paper that the Queen's Own had arrived in Toronto and had been disbanded, as the Fenian eruption seemed to be over. After this, he had no reason to go to Toronto and therefore determined to return immediately to Parry Sound.

The skirmish at Ridgeway was short-lived and the Fenians retreated, but this event caused the Province of Canada to recognize the country's vulnerability to attack. The Government immediately increased military appropriations, and the militia was reorganized. There was also a greater sense of urgency in the Province's talks with the other British North American colonies about political union. New Brunswick, in particular, supported Confederation, as it was especially vulnerable to attack from the

11

United States. The following year, in 1867, New Brunswick, Nova Scotia, and the Province of Canada (as Ontario and Quebec) entered into Confederation.

John's return from Collingwood to Parry Sound turned into a hair-raising adventure. Galbraith paid an Indian five dollars to take him from Collingwood across Georgian Bay in a group with eight other Indian men and one woman. They had three boats and were headed for Christian Island, a distance of twenty miles. They started out at 8 p.m. and reached the Island a little after sunrise. Many of the party were drinking and the man he had hired to take him all the way to Parry Sound did not want to continue. He was finally persuaded and assured John he would be alright once the whiskey was out of him.

It took another day and a half for Galbraith and his guide to reach Parry Sound. When the wind was good, John made a sail out of the Indian's blanket. During the trip, as he was accustomed to do while travelling with Indians, John added to his Ojibwa vocabulary. They arrived at Moose Point, eighteen miles from Christian Island at sundown, and camped for the night. The following day the two men had breakfast and then started out on the last twenty miles to Parry Sound. On the way John attempted to shoot a loon and a duck, but the gun did not go off because the powder was wet. The two men landed in early afternoon, and John paid his guide and returned to camp. Everyone was astonished to see him. The next day he was back at work as usual. One of the Indian guides remarked that it was a miracle his canoe was not swamped in the open water because of the rough weather.

In his diary John portrayed the difficulties faced by a surveyor in that part of Ontario. The landscape was rugged, dotted liberally with lakes and rivers, and covered with virgin forests of maple, birch, cedar, and pine. The cry of the loon echoed on the lonely lakes at night. It was not uncommon for a man to spear more than twenty-five fish in the space of an hour.

The usual means of transportation to and from camp was by canoe, with Indians acting as guides. A birch-bark canoe was the most efficient type of craft for this purpose, particularly because of its light weight. A man could carry a small canoe on his shoulders and portage from one river to another. The early fur traders had used the same type of craft, which they had copied from the Indian. On this particular survey, John Peters, one of the Indian guides, got bark to make a canoe for himself.

To make a canoe the Indians peeled large strips of bark from white birch trees in the spring, when the bark was moist. They sewed the pieces together with strips of leather thonging and then fastened them around a framework of light spruce wood. The whole was supported by a framework of stakes driven into the ground during construction. Pitch or melted gum was used to seal the seams and make the canoe waterproof. In such a craft an Indian could paddle for hours without sound or fatigue, never raising his paddle from the water.

The surveyors themselves walked from their camp sites through the bush to the survey sites; because the territory was rugged and unmarked, they frequently got lost. Their enemies, the black flies and sand flies, often drove them to shelter during the day, and at night hordes of vicious mosquitoes disturbed their sleep. One morning it took John and his partner until eleven o'clock to reach their work site, and they did not get back to camp until eleven that evening. John was determined to get that particular piece of work finished and decided that they should camp on the site, which meant carrying all their provisions for several days, as well as all the survey equipment.

The Foley survey was finished on Friday, July 27, at 3 p.m., and the men prepared for an early start for home the following morning. Their heavy gear was taken to Parry Sound by the Indians and sent from there by steamer. The surveyors themselves set out in three canoes. To reach Lake Joseph, they made eight portages and travelled twenty miles. At McCabe's Bay they hired a team to carry the canoes to the Severn River, thirteen miles away. That night they camped at the Indian village on Lake Couchiching, where again they hired a team to carry the canoes and traps from the Talbot River on Lake Simcoe to Balsam Lake. They paddled through gale-force winds on Balsam, Cameron, and Sturgeon Lakes. At Bridgemouth, near Bobcaygeon, the men parted, and George Stewart, John Peters, and John Galbraith walked into Peterborough and caught the train to Port Hope. The trip had taken five days from the survey site, and the men had paddled or portaged 136 miles.

On this survey, as on others, John Galbraith had spent his spare moments reading and studying. He added to his knowledge of Indian dialects. John Peters was an Ojibwa, who taught John his dialect. Galbraith always carried a notebook with him, to write down phrases, grammar, and single words. His interest in their customs and his attempt to converse with them in their own tongue endeared him to the Indians, and throughout his life he was always provided with the best Indian guides when he travelled in the bush. John Peters became a close friend.

John's years as a student seemed to him to pass quickly. He studied Mathematics, English, French, German, Italian, Spanish, Chemistry, Mineralogy, Geology, History, and Ethnology. His final goal remained engineering, but languages were also important to him. He wanted to be able to read scientific papers published in other countries. Eventually he was able to read or speak thirteen different languages, including several Indian tongues. During the summer holidays he worked in the bush and continued to learn Cree and Ojibwa from his Indian guides.

During his student years his father occasionally stopped to visit him. After one visit on October 27, 1868 he wrote a letter to his mother telling her that he had taken his father to one of his Society meetings to give him a idea of student life. He also asked her to send several books with him the next time he came – La Bruyer and Molière. He went on to say that:

Convocation has been put off till the 16th. If you are coming try to be up then. A memorial window in honour of those killed at Ridgeway is being made and Convocation has been postponed until it is finished. . . . I was received into the membership of the church on Wednesday evening. Tomorrow I shall sit at the Lord's table for the first time. I feel as if I could say no more on this subject it is so new to me to write this. Pray for me, dear Mother, that I may be enabled to live a truly Christian life and that no one may be prevented from coming to Christ through my failing.

John graduated in 1868 from University College with a Bachelor of Arts (B.A.) degree. He won the gold medal in Mathematics, first class honours in Modern Languages and Natural History, and the Prince of Wales Prize.

After graduation John Galbraith moved back to Port Hope and began an apprenticeship with his old friend George Stewart, now Chief Engineer of the Midland Railway and later of the Grand Trunk. He worked with Stewart on the construction of the road from Peterborough to Lakefield, on the survey of the extension from Lindsay to Beaverton, and on many other land surveys in the area.

John gained engineering experience while maintaining his contact with the University. In 1869 he was appointed to the Engineering staff of the Intercolonial Railway. He worked on construction eastward from Rivière du Loup until September 1870, when he became Contractors' Engineer for Section 18, in the Matapedia Valley, where he stayed until September 1871. In that month the Midland Railway appointed him Resident Engineer on its extension from Beaverton to Orillia; after that portion was finished, he was in charge of construction from Orillia to Georgian Bay, which was stopped in 1874.

During the next few months in order to increase his understanding of engineering in all its facets, he spent some time visiting U.S. engineering works and schools. Besides the Rolling Mills, Portland, Maine, he visited the Locomotive Works, Philadelphia and the Phoenixville Iron and Bridge Works, Phoenixville, Pennsylvania. He was also given the opportunity to visit the United States Navy Yard in Charlestown. He visited the School of Mines, Columbia College, New York, and the Stevens Institute, a school of mechanical and civil Engineering, in Hoboken, N.J.

Upon his return, until the spring of 1875 when he returned to Portland, he went into private practice in Port Hope, during which time he received his Master of Arts from the University of Toronto. He had by now been appointed Examiner in Mathematics for the University. In 1874–75 he was Examiner in Mathematics and Civil Engineering. When the survey of the International Boundary between Canada and the United States was begun, he was asked to be one of the four Canadian Astronomical Assistants, but due to other commitments did not accept. In 1877 and in 1878 he was Examiner in Civil Engineering.

Because he wanted to learn more about mechanical engineering, he had returned to Portland and become a mechanical draftsman in the Portland Co. (Locomotive Works). This firm also manufactured stationary and marine engines, grain elevator works, and general machinery. In November, 1875, while in Portland, he was offered the post of Division Engineer, Eastern Division, Georgian Bay Branch, Canadian Pacific Railway (C.P.R.). He accepted the job and stayed until the close of the Parliamentary Session of 1876, when the contract terminated. The following June the Government sent him as an assistant to Thomas Ridout, Esq., C.E., in an Exploratory Survey for the C.P.R. from French River to Vermilion Lake.

John Galbraith was thirty-two years of age in 1878. His private practice included waterworks, mills, water-power, and architecture. In each area he read extensively. During these years he received diplomas as Provincial Land Surveyor, Dominion Land Surveyor, and Passed Candidate in Higher Surveying. This last diploma was given by the Dominion Government. He was accepted as Associate of the Institution of Civil Engineers, London, England, an institution that was one of the most important of its kind in the world.

For recreation, John turned to his love of canoeing and roughing it outdoors. In 1877 he and his friend John Peters camped on the banks of the Wye River, near Midland, and tried to solve a seventeenth-century mystery. It was there that French priests had established a mission among the Hurons about 1640. In 1649 the neighbouring missions at Sturgeon Bay and Victoria were burnt by the Mohawks, and the missionaries Brébeuf and Lalemant were martyred.

These attacks occurred in March, but the Mohawks did not attack Ste. Marie. By the following June, the missionaries at Ste. Marie had reason to fear that they might be next, and so they burned the mission and started out with their Huron friends in boats, down the Wye River, heading toward Georgian Bay, and Christian Island, site of an Indian settlement. The Wye was shallow and wended its way through marshy ground into Georgian Bay. It was relatively easy to paddle through the reeds without detection, and it was equally easy for a hostile tribe to attack without warning. On their way down this river, according to the story that John Peters told Galbraith, the missionaries landed and buried their silver service on the bank and to mark the spot planted a young hemlock tree, which they had brought from their fort. They sent a message back to France describing the site, and more than 200 years later, in 1863, some Jesuits came from France, found this tree, cut it down, dug up the silver, and carried it away.

After breaking camp, Galbraith told Peters that he wanted to find the place. About a quarter-mile above the mouth of the river, they saw a rotten tree lying in the wake and paddled over to it. Peters, breaking off the rotten bark, told him that it was a hemlock. Galbraith examined the roots, which were on the bank, and found that they had been cut by an axe and also found marks of digging. He was sure that this was the tree planted in 1649, because it was the only hemlock there, and so he carried off the roots, which he took home to his mother. He made sketches of the site, which are now in the museum at Ville Ste. Marie.

CHAPTER THREE

Professor – "for the love of it"

URING THE 1870S, when John Galbraith was in private practice and gaining wide experience, talks had been going on among provincial officials regarding the training of engineers. Canada needed qualified men for the rapidly expanding railway systems, roads, and bridges. Vast mineral and natural resources were still untapped. In the mid–1870s France and England had recognized the need for training engineers; despite much opposition from those who had gained their expertise through apprenticeship, both countries opened technical schools. Technical colleges were springing up in the United States as part of existing universities or as separate entities. In New Brunswick, the first lectures in Engineering were given in 1853; a few years later, at McGill University in Montreal, several courses in the Practical Sciences were offered. Interest was growing as a result of the 1851 Exhibition in London, and thoughtful men were recognizing the need for training in Canada. Members of the Legislative Assembly of United Canada and of the Senate of the University of Toronto continued to discuss the problem.

Engineering and related areas were considered a trade in those days. A university was an academic institution where a mere trade had no place, and far-sighted men realized that this had to change. The question was, should existing facilities at the University be used, or a separate institution built? Should a college train only operating technicians and mechanics, or should its instruction be academic?

In 1871 the Provincial Government issued a circular addressed to the "Manufacturers of Ontario," stating that the object of the proposed "School of Industrial Science" was "to provide, in a two-fold form, for the education of Mining and Civil and Mechanical Engineers; of Manipulation in Metals; of Workers in Wood, Leather, Woolen and Flax Fibres; of Designers, Modellers and Carvers in the Decorative and Industrial Arts; and of persons desirous of studying Chemistry, as applied to our various Manufacturers."

Time went on, with no decision made about the location of the proposed School, or the curriculum. One stumbling block was having two groups of professors, at the University and at the proposed School, teaching similar subjects. In 1871 McGill appointed a Professor of Civil Engineering and also a Lecturer in Assaying and Mining in the Department of Applied Science, within its Faculty of Arts. To many, Toronto would be foolish to do otherwise. Another difficulty that surfaced, particularly in New Brunswick, was the shortage of qualified surveyors. These men worked during the good weather and lectured when it was impossible to work out-of-doors.

The controversy continued until the opening of the Legislature in 1871. The Lieutenant Governor announced that a new School of Technology would open shortly, to prepare skilled men as engineers, managers, and operators in the various mechanical and manufacturing establishments and in the steamboat and railway systems of the country. On May 6, 1872, the School of Technology opened in downtown Toronto, with evening classes from 7.45 until 9, five days a week. Admission was free, but by ticket only. Drawing, Natural Philosophy, and Chemistry were taught. Most of the students were mechanics who worked during the day. Its status was temporary, and its courses were haphazard.

In March 1873 the Act to Establish a School of Practical Science passed. According to the Act, the School "was to be in Ontario, for instruction in mining engineering and the mechanical and manufacturing arts. In connection with it there was to be a museum of geology and mineralogy, with other branches, in order to afford aids for practical instruction and illustrations of the mineral and economic products of the Province." This School was to be under control of the Lieutenant-Governor-in-Council, with internal management delegated to a Board or Council composed of lecturers and instructors. The Act was introduced by Adam Crooks, who was vitally interested in education. He had been a member of the Senate of the University for many years, acting as Vice-Chancellor for a time, and in 1871 was elected as a Liberal member of the Legislative Assembly of Ontario. In 1873 he became Provincial Treasurer.

James Loudon, Professor of Mathematics at the University, lectured for the evening classes at the School of Technology and was now a member of the Senate of the University. His original feeling was that lectures in the new School of Practical Science ought to be supplemented by other courses at University College, and the Library and University Museum used by both. Adam Crooks, in his report to the Legislature in 1873, advised that the downtown site of the School of Technology be sold and a new building constructed close to the University. James Loudon agreed; he thought that the professional school and University College could share a library and geological museum.

In 1874, the School of Technology still offered evening classes only, to artisans, mechanics, and workmen. Interest had climbed and enrolment increased, but the existing arrangements left the School of Technology unable to fulfil its original aims. Professor Loudon undertook to prepare a report for the Provincial Treasurer, recommending an uptown school. Under the heading of Engineering – which included Civil, Mechanical, and Mining – he recommended at least five professors, to instruct in Drawing, Mathematics, Applied Mechanics, Surveying, Assaying, Metallurgy, and Civil Engineering. Also, there must be provision for the study of the Physical Sciences. He believed that the Mechanics' Institute was still the proper place for artisans to improve their skills. He suggested a budget that he thought the province could live with, as well as a simple plan for extending the activities of the proposed School of Practical Science into professional education. The plan was accepted, but still no action was taken. By this time Loudon had more responsibilities at the University and no longer had time for his lectures at the School of Technology.

The status of the proposed School was hotly debated in the Legislature, and the final decision was to sell the downtown building back to the Mechanics' Institute for $28,000.00. The Government planned to put the money into a new building on university grounds and set aside $5,600.00 for the salaries of the professors to be hired.

In June 1878, the building on the University grounds that became known and loved as the Little Red School House was almost ready for occupancy. Professors for Chemistry, Mining Engineering, Natural Philosphy, and Biology were already appointed. Only the most important position on the staff, that of Professor of Engineering, remained unfilled. The position had been promised in the spring to a Montreal engineer, and he had travelled to Toronto and made suggestions about the set-up of classrooms in the new building; but because of strong opposition to the method of appointment, the position was thrown open to competition. Advertisements appeared in the press as well as several English scientific journals, offering a Chair of Civil Engineering at the new School of Practical Science (S.P.S.). There were nine applicants, of whom five were from England and Ireland. John Galbraith was one of the nine, and in the late summer he submitted his application, along with his testimonials and recommendations.

Galbraith's professional qualifications were excellent, and he had ten years of practical experience. His appearance was against him, because he was short, slow of speech, and had an occasional lisp, but he was a man of great and balanced strength. He received the appointment – a decision, James Loudon later said, "most fortunate for the future of engineering in Canada."

The appointment was not made until September 28, and so John Galbraith was not at the first meeting of the School's Board, on October 1. He did attend the next meeting, on October 5, but his name did not even appear on the calendar for that year. The Board, appointed by the Lieutenant Governor, consisted of six people, H.H. Croft, Professor of Chemistry; E.J. Chapman, Professor of Mineralogy and Geology; James Loudon, Professor of Mathematics and Natural Philosophy; R. Ramsay Wright, Professor of Biology; John Galbraith, Professor of Engineering; and

21

W.H. Ellis, Assistant to the Professor of Chemistry. Ellis had been on the staff of the School of Technology and had acted as its principal.

The first students at S.P.S. were admitted on the basis of their practical experience, and they hoped to obtain diplomas after a three-year course of study. The Engineering Course was set up by the first Minister of Education in Ontario, Adam Crooks, who followed many of the ideas put forth by the professor of Mathematics, James Loudon, of University College. The first-year courses were common to every student. In his second year the student decided whether his interest were Civil, Mining, or Mechanical, and from then on he specialized in his chosen field. One of the first men to arrive to enrol wanted to take up boxing. In his mind it was a "practical science."

John Galbraith started off with seven students and was compelled to follow the course of studies set out by the Board of Education. Because the new School was so late in starting, there was no time for the students to sit for entrance exams, and therefore only those with previous practical experience were accepted. The following year, Galbraith designed the course according to his theories of what an engineer should know, and also "to afford the necessary preliminary preparation to students intending to enter the various professional branches of engineering." Either French or German was added, because the French and Germans were very active scientifically and their papers were not published in English. Galbraith was an accomplished linguist and found it helpful to be able to read data published in non-English-speaking countries.

He taught all the engineering subjects and also gave practical field instruction in Surveying and Astronomy. He was also solely responsible for the work in Drawing, Structural and Mechanical Design, Mapping, and Topography. On top of that, he taught a course in the evening on the Theory of the Steam Engine to artisans, mechanics, and workmen. There were fourteen courses in all, but, as he frequently said, "The work was the same for ten students as for twenty." He requested a Fellow in Engineering to help him, but because of budget allocations got no one until 1884, when he had a graduate student to help. There were not even suitable textbooks as references; he therefore prepared and wrote out all his lectures, based on his own reading and experience. These lectures are now preserved in the U. of T. Archives of the John P. Robarts Library at the University of Toronto.

In 1884 the University of Toronto's Senate inaugurated a professional degree of Civil Engineer, under certain conditions, available to graduates of the School of Practical Science (S.P.S.). Until then a man customarily added C.E. to his name when he reached the rank of Assistant Engineer in a project, without any examination or diploma from a recognized authority. With the establishment of this degree, the Department of Civil Engineering in University College closed down. Galbraith had never been impressed with the department because it contained no technological subjects. The Arts course in Mathematics and Science was far superior.

Late in 1884 one of the second-year students at the School, T. Kennard Thompson, later an outstanding engineer in New York City, invited John Galbraith, all the second- and third-year students, W.H. Ellis, the Assistant to the Professor of Chemistry, and several others to his place to discuss formation of an undergraduate engineering society. Galbraith approved the idea, and by the following March the first Engineering Society in Canada was in full swing. Galbraith agreed to take on the Presidency until it was firmly established. Four years later he felt he was no longer needed, and the first student President, H.T.H. Haultain, took over.

At the University John had far too much work to do justice to it. He taught all the courses, with only one graduate student to help.

There is no other engineering school in the world where such a variety of work is thrown on one professor as in the School of Practical Science.

I still concentrate on Civil Engineering and pay special attention to areas where the young engineer has little or no help from his superiors on the job.

Each year more applications come from students who wish to be Mechanical Engineers. We do not have either the staff or the laboratory space. It is an important field and must be provided for. I now give all the lectures except for a few in first year, supervise part of the practical work in Drawing and Surveying, perform the duties of a dean and registrar, carry on all correspondence requiring professional knowledge, and generally administer the affairs of the Department. Because we are educating engineers not merely mechanical tradesmen there are no texts to fall back on and I must thoroughly investigate every aspect of every course I teach.

My staff must be large enough so that an instructor can be a specialist in his area. I ought not to have to teach Astronomy to one class and the Theory of the Steam Engine to the next — I tell the story of a hypothetical engineer who is in a much worse situation than a Professor of Chemistry and Botany from Oxford. When he visited the foreign chemist he introduced himself as a Professor of Botany; when visiting the botanist he became a Professor of Chemistry.

He told his students that he "did not plan to turn out full fledged engineers and it was farcial to give a boy a degree of Civil Engineering at the end of three years." His goal was to teach a man how to study, so that in later years, by careful study and hard practical experience, he could teach himself to be a capable engineer. He advised a man not to take a permanent position the day he graduated, but to move around for ten years or so, working in various fields, until he discovered what it was he was best suited for. "There is nothing," he wrote, "so sad as a square peg in a round hole." He also advised a young engineer to secure an increase in salary with every move, on the principle that the higher the salary the better the experience, since an employer can be depended upon to give the most important work to the best-paid man.

Because of lack of laboratory space Galbraith delivered lectures from October to April and expected his students to take a job in some field of engineering during the other months. When students returned in the fall, they were required to turn in a thesis on some practical issue of their summer work. Understandably, this was not popular, as he expected this thesis to be done in great detail, complete with maps and drawings, and it constituted part of their term marks. He felt also that they needed a change from the classroom environment. Besides giving his students an opportunity to put theory into practice, the break gave Galbraith time to visit other institutions to update his own knowledge and to indulge his love of the wilderness.

Over the years, in developing the curriculum for the School of Practical Science (S.P.S.), John Galbraith put his thoughts on paper and filed them away for future use. His aim in the education of an engineer was to teach him to read for himself. "Too many subjects make a student a Jack of all trades and a master of none." Galbraith's plan was to give formal instruction in what would be useful to the engineer but was not easy to learn in ordinary practice. Mathematics, Physics, and Chemistry as applied in engineering were the basic subjects. These were broad terms and were broken down into descriptive geometry, engineering statics and dynamics, strength and elasticity of materials, thermodynamics, and hydraulics.

In a three- or four-year course it was necessary to select carefully the portions of the general sciences to be taught. These should lead as quickly as possible to the object aimed at by the scientific professions. Hence study of outside conditions could save classroom time. John considered no knowledge useless to the engineer, but not all knowledge could be taught – only methods of attack and knowledge of materials. The engineer had to be able in addition to judge workmanship and be familiar with the products of the various trades. A student also required some knowledge of business and law.

Galbraith considered languages essential. French and German enabled an engineer to keep abreast of developments abroad, but English was most important of all. An engineer had to be able to express himself clearly and suitably in English. It was not possible during the term to spend much time on English essays hence Galbraith's emphasis on daily journals on the summer job.

As a result of all this, the curriculum was becoming badly congested. With the increase in student numbers came more instructors, buildings, and equipment and specialization of subjects. John was concerned that the instruction was given in such detail that the wearied student lost his grasp. One remedy was to give options, but this meant increasing the number of courses and complications in the timetable. The timetable was already congested – "like the curriculum and the brains of the students."

Some members of staff felt that reducing the number of subjects would give students more time to waste. John stated that it might as well be wasted as not. He thought that all laboratory records should be made in laboratory time, with evenings left free:

Studious men will utilize them in study. Encourage the men inclined to be studious and do not discourage men who want to learn. The whole tendency of the present system is to discourage thought and encourage cram. The lecturer cannot be prevented from using the time allotted to him in teaching at high pressure, in teaching as if his were the only subject in the curriculum. There would not be much objection to this if the number of subjects were reduced. The time gained could be used in examining the classes, testing their knowledge and finding out and explaining their difficulties. Night work should be reduced to a minimum as it consists largely in preparing records of the laboratory work.

Galbraith saw no difficulty in limiting night work to a few experiments:

Except for the art of cramming and of sizing up the peculiarities of the examiners one of the great dangers of a long academic course is that it trains probably so fine the habits and modes of thought that the student may be made unfit for the rough conflict and ready decisions which form a great part of his professional life. The enjoyment of academic life may sap his strength and energy. A man should be thrown into the world while he is young and before he becomes stale. Men who survive the first half dozen years of academia may become good professors but may be comparatively poor engineers. The academy cultivates in men the critical and analysing match of thought but is apt to destroy performance. One cannot become a strong swimmer without going into the water. Most of our successful men are unbalanced men. The balanced thinker will never do anything worth while. Thus it is not good to know too much. We give our students too much but they do not take in what we give them. Nature develops in them the proper anti-toxin.

He thought that it would be good for students if their professors could alternate three years of extramural work with three years intramural work throughout their careers.

The university is a little world dependent on the big world for its support but should not be a parasite. It should by its works make the big world feel that it is worth-while. The student who wishes to make the most of his time must work hard at what ever he has to do, whether it be sport, societies, study or passing examinations. The idler is the bane of the little world as well as of the big one and neither has any use for him, and it is because we have had so many workers and so few idlers that our graduates have gained the recognition of the country which puts up the money for their training.

The man is indeed fortunate who earns his living in a calling which he would pursue if he were a millionaire as for example the caddy, the professor, the prizefighter, the preacher, for I can't imagine anyone entering these professions under the pressure of necessity, and besides there is no money in them. The man who adopts the profession of an engineer from the love of it belongs to the same class. He will probably earn a decent living and get as much enjoyment out of life as the millionaire.

There is no use in assuming that a man makes a sacrifice in becoming a professor or an engineer or in entering any vocation from the love of it and without the compulsion of necessity or in assuming that if he had liked he might have been a millionaire. Both assumptions are probably incorrect and belong rather to the regions of fancy than reason and are like the existence of the fourth dimension incapable of proof, all honest men not competent, all competent men not honest.

CHAPTER FOUR

Northern Adventure

ONE SPRING MORNING in 1881 John Galbraith was chatting in his office with a friend who inquired about his plans for the summer. A map of Canada hung on the wall, and half in fun, half in earnest, John said that he would go to Lake Superior, get a canoe and Indian guides, ascend the Michipicoten River to the height of land, descend the Moose to Moose Factory, coast along James Bay to Rupert House, ascend Rupert River to Lake Mistassini, and from there get into Lake St. John and paddle down the Saguenay to Tadoussac.

The idea took root. The more he thought about it, the more enthusiastic he became and the more determined to make the effort. He talked to friends in the Hudson's Bay Company and with his usual thoroughness began planning in earnest. In Toronto he purchased enough supplies to get him to Moose Factory, including tea and tobacco as presents for the Indians. He packed a tent, blankets, cooking utensils, a Winchester carbine, fishing gear, a small pocket compass, a pocket sextant, a glass artificial horizon, a nautical almanac, and maps. He had banknotes in a waterproof belt and the latest English, Canadian, and American newspapers, which would be welcome at Company posts in the north.

Equally as important were letters of introduction to officers in the Hudson's Bay Company's service. In those regions a man depended on the goodwill of the Company's officers for Indian guides, canoes, and provisions, and if the officers felt they were dealing with a fur trader they were apt to be not as obliging. Fur traders, both Indian and white, took the beaver pelts they had trapped to sell and trade to the Hudson's Bay Posts. Rivers and lakes were the highways between the isolated forts and civilization. Steamers plodded up the Great Lakes to Superior, taking flour, sugar, tools, mail, and other necessities to the scattered communities en route. New employees of the Company, from both Canada and England, went by steamer to the rivers; there they transferred to canoes, which carried them, with their letters of introduction and all their belongings, to new homes in the wilderness.

These waterways were busy and colourful. Company men travelled in brigades, generally a party of twenty or more, in three long birch-bark canoes. They carried mail, instructions, and business letters in waterproof packages for the factors (managers) in the outlying posts. Indians acted as guides, portaging goods and canoes and setting up camps, and were often accompanied by their women, children, and dogs. Parties of Indians moved from one camp to another, hunting and fishing, and could be seen regularly letting down their nets into waters teeming with fish. Game was plentiful, and the Indians often feasted on bear meat or beaver, but they had to carry necessities, such as flour, tea, and tobacco, with them. The forts were their lifeline.

The waterways provided a social network between communities. Gossip was exchanged and news passed on of events elsewhere. Some Indians paddled in small canoes, carrying messages from one fort to another; others had canoes full of bundles of furs to exchange for money or goods. These trips took days, because of the distances between posts. The rivers were fast and treacherous, and the men made many portages. Sometimes the canoes had to be completely emptied, and all the goods plus the canoe had to be carried, perhaps miles, across land from one body of water to another. If the water were shallow and rocky, the men used long poles and carefully poled the canoe through. In other places the canoe was tracked and lightened as much as necessary, and then lines were attached to the bow and stern. The men could then walk along the shore and pull their canoes into safer waters. If the wind were right, travellers hoisted a sail and made good time. Time was measured by the number of days it took to paddle from one spot to another, and there were many well-used camp sites along the shores. Often two or three groups camped together and shared

29

gossip, goods, and camaraderie. No one paddled these waters for the sheer joy and adventure – no one, that is, except John Galbraith.

Galbraith left Toronto on June 10, 1881 on the Grand Trunk Railway for Sarnia, where he boarded the steamer *Manitoba*. En route, the *Manitoba* stopped at Southampton, the Ducks, Bruce Mines, and several other places; it arrived in drizzly rain at Sault Ste. Marie, where John purchased potatoes and reading material. At the next stop, the Caribou Islands, he met a Mr. Bowman, a Hudson Bay factor, whom he was to meet again at the end of his journey. The following day the ship docked at Silver Inlet, where John visited with two men to whom he had letters of introduction, Dr. Campbell and Captain Tretheway.

The next port-of-call was Prince Arthur's Landing (now Thunder Bay), on Lake Superior, where John put up at Mrs. Flaherty's, as the steamer was in port for several days. While there, seven of the passengers hired a rig and drove to nearby Fort William, where they looked through the town. John invited several men to have tea with him and obtained refraction tables from one of them.

Six days after leaving Sarnia, the *Manitoba* arrived at Red Rock. The following day John rowed up the river to the Hudson's Bay · post, where he bought a three-fathom canoe from Mr. Reynolds for $16.00. The following day the *Manitoba* arrived at Pie River and delivered the freight for the Hudson's Bay post there. About 11 p.m. the steamer reached the Michipicoten River where John disembarked. He met Mr. Kirkpatrick from Missinaibi and Mr. Bell, who was very friendly and assured him that he and his wife would be pleased to have him take his meals with them. Bell provided him with a map of his route to Moose Factory, had a man work on his canoe, and found a half-breed, Ashtakeeghig, to act as guide and an Indian, Windigoons, as cook for him.

On Tuesday, June 21, Galbraith settled his account with Bell, gave him his letters for home, and said good-bye. He and his guides started up the river at 6 a.m. and on the long portage overtook Bowman and his four men and the Hudson's Bay Brigade of twenty men with three canoes. They all camped at the upper end of the portage, which was about three miles long. There were also three or four other Indians; (thence) thirty in all camped there. In his diary John labels the camp number 1 and notes that they paddled about thirteen miles that day.

The following day the groups parted. Bowman gave John the parcels and letters for Moose Factory. John did not expect to see either Bowman or the Hudson's Bay brigade again. Ashtakeeghig was sick and so he had to engage another guide. They got away about 8 a.m. and made two portages before noon. They tracked the canoe up the first portage, but Windigoons and Jimmy, the new man, walked it upstream at the second, and they landed for dinner at noon. They started out again at 1.30 and camped for the night at 6 p.m. The currents were very strong all day, but John estimated that they made about fifteen miles. The next day they started out about 4.45 a.m. in cloudy weather, and Windigoons forgot his paddle. (Another time an axe was left behind and also John's precious cane.) They worked up to Cat Portage through a very strong current about a mile and a half above where they camped the previous night. At one point Jimmy caught sight of a bear going up the hill. During the afternoon they reached Manitowik Lake, which was about two miles wide and ten miles long. They camped there for the night and had a visit from an Indian family. These types of activities formed the pattern of their days.

The next day they reached Dog Lake, an intricate lake, and paddled by many turns, points, bays, and islands. On the points, especially on Dog Lake, they saw many bears' skulls painted with red bands and hanging on poles partly painted red. About 3.30 p.m. they arrived at the Height of Land Portage, in a tamarac swamp approximately 300 yards long, dividing the waters flowing into Lake Superior from those falling into Hudson Bay. It took a full hour to get everything (back) into the canoe and start on Crooked Lake, the headwater of the north branch of the Moose River.

The country through which they were paddling was wet and low, and the hills were small. Mosquitoes swarmed and caused great discomfort, especially at night. At one point Ashtakeeghig, who had recovered, took the bow and had not been there for more than an hour when they ran on a rock, fortunately without damage. Five days after leaving Michipicoten they reached the Missinaibi Post on

31

Lake Missinaibi. When the factor, Mr. Kirkpatrick, saw them coming, he ran up the Hudson's Bay Company flag. John found him busy trading with Indians. Everyone there had a cough, they called the "epigoot," and which seemed to John similar to whooping cough. A short time later a Mr. Brown arrived in another canoe, bringing the axe and paddle that had been left behind. They all spent a pleasant evening under a clear sky, and Kirkpatrick discovered a very fine comet in the north.

Sunday was clear and sunny, and so John spent some time taking observations and found his watch seventeen minutes and fifty-one seconds ahead of Toronto time. He had two watches with him, one set on Toronto time and the other set according to the sun at midday, which he compared. John left Ashtakeeghig and Jimmy to return to their homes and hired another man, Peter. Rain delayed their departure until early Tuesday. They passed twelve rapids and ran most of them but had to lighten the canoe for some and walk over two or three portages. Windigoons was rather sulky, even though John had advanced him three dollars because he had not brought a third man along.

Thundering Water rapids were exciting. Windigoons and Peter took the lightened canoe over them and almost lost it. They broke one paddle, lost another, which was knocked out of Peter's hands, and broke a pole. That night they camped about three miles below St. Paul's Portage; Windigoons and Peter took "pot" (probably alcohol) and threatened to desert, but in the morning they thought better of it. They slept hardly a wink because of the mosquitoes and started off in the morning in rain. They were in level water nearly all that day and ran only four rapids. Twice in succession they scraped the rocks, the first time such a thing had happened with Windigoons in the bow. The way was very crooked, and Windigoons could barely see because of the spray in his face. The countryside was rugged. The principal trees seen from the river were spruce, tamarac, poplar, balm of gilead, birch, and balsam; the banks were clay in many places.

The waters of the Missinaibi River became much more difficult, with more rapids and rocks, and the canoe was scraped badly several times. Repairs and rain slowed progress. While his men were repairing the canoe, John took observations for longitude and latitude.

On July 3 they arrived at the Store Portage, named for an old Hudson's Bay store-house, which once stood at the beginning of the portage. Alongside was a neatly fenced-in Indian grave – the first building they had seen since leaving the Missinaibi Post. The walls and beams had the names and dates of travellers up and down the river carved on them. The oldest inscription he saw was James Garson, 1840. He saw also the names of Thompson and Maddock, who had had such a hard time getting up the river without Indians in October 1879. He left his name and those of the two Indians.

The country was isolated. The soil was generally light-coloured clay, and the rivers were full of rocks and shoals. Several times they scraped the canoe. They ran into a group of Wahbushkong making canoes and fishing, the first people they had seen since leaving Missinaibi. They also saw caribou and wild geese, which they tried unsuccessfully to shoot. Another day brought them to the junction of the Moose River and the Abittibee. The demarcation between these two waters was very distinct: the Abittibee's water was turbid, a light clay colour; the Moose's transparent reddish brown. Broken pieces of limestone all along the beach were full of fossils.

They arrived in Moose Factory a day later than John had expected. Mr. Cotter, the factor, met them at the landing, where John presented his letters of introduction and was kindly received. Cotter spent the afternoon showing him around the place. Later, John met the clerks, McKay, Mason, and Gillis, and Dr. Haydon. He was given a room in the clerks' house and took his meals at the mess, while his men used the tent. In the evening he met Mrs. Cotter and Mrs. Haydon. Kirkpatrick's men from the Missinaibi Post arrived the same night. The following day John paid off his guides, Windigoons ($18.00) and Peter ($19.00), and enjoyed the company of the other men. Cotter and Haydon gave him a number of photos of the area.

In the evening the doctor and his wife invited Galbraith to supper, and they sat up until about 1 a.m. chatting. Next morning John prepared to leave. The wind was good, and he was anxious to get to Rupert House before the schooner left there for Moose, so that he could send his men back by it. Cotter found two Muskegon as guides, John and Edward, who appeared to be good men. Mrs. Cotter put a loaf of bread and a jar of butter among his things. He wrote his letters before leaving, and Cotter gave him letters to carry to Mr. McTavish at Rupert House and to the gentlemen in charge of the post on Lake St. John, Quebec. The British and the Hudson's Bay Company flags were run up as a send-off.

John made his seventeenth camp that night. His observation for latitude showed them to be 51° 16′ 12″ N, with high water at 2.10 p.m. They were stranded for several days because of rain and high winds. John worried that if they did not make Rupert House within a couple of days they would be out of flour. To his chagrin, he discovered that four hams had been left behind. He had no option but to send one of his men back by land. He also sent a request to Cotter for 12 lb. of pork, in case the hams had been stolen, 24 lb. of flour, and 2 lb. of sugar. Toward evening the man arrived back by canoe, bringing along his son. He had found three of the hams; one had been taken by an animal. He also brought the supplies that John had ordered, along with letters from Cotter and another loaf of bread and jar of butter from his wife.

John now had a crew of three and was able to make better time. The country was becoming flatter, like a prairie, and low trees could be seen in the distance. They passed the mouth of the Hannah Bay River a few miles from the site of the old Hudson's Bay fort. Galbraith's small party camped for breakfast a short distance up the Paskepolahshe River, and because the wind was rising John ordered his tent pitched. His men went out shooting and returned with twenty ducks before heavy wind and rain nearly blew the tent over. The storm was so severe that the river overflowed the camp site and forced the men to bundle everything into the canoe and start in the middle of the storm for a new camping ground, about a mile up the river. Two of his men had developed bad colds, and John doctored them with pain-killer and then made them sleep in his tent.

He used this pain-killer more than once and mentioned that he gave a dose to an Indian baby who was screaming, to no effect. At other times, if the Indians had worked especially hard and were exhausted, he handed out a dose. His remedy would no doubt be similar to Davis' Pain Killer, a popular patent medicine of the time. Davis's remedy containing 1/2 lb. of powdered opium, 1 lb. of caustic liquor of ammonia, 6 lb. of cayenne pepper, 2 lb. of camphor, and 20 lb. of powdered guaiacum. This was all mixed with 32 gallons of alcohol, allowed to sit for two weeks, and then filtered.

As James Bay flowed into Hannah Bay they were now able to swim in salt water and one day were delighted to see two white porpoises swimming nearby. There were numerous ducks and an unusual bird, known in Cree as Pahpahgpitasoo, that made a noise exactly like striking two sticks together. They could see Rupert House across Rupert Bay estimated by John to be seven miles away. As they were out of provisions, John persuaded his men, against their will, to start across. The currents of two large rivers, the Rupert and the Nahtowa, met the tide-water in Rupert Bay, which made a rough crossing; it took two hours of hard paddling with the sail up to reach the post. John was interested in the topography, which had changed from level prairie with high grass to a wooded and rocky shoreline.

There were very few Indians at Rupert House, because the brigades for Mistassini, Neechkoon, and Waswonaby had started up the river about a week earlier. McTavish, the factor, was able to get two men, old Namagoons as guide and Longback as cook, for the trip to Mistassini. These two men immediately started work, patching up the canoe, battered by a journey of more than 450 miles. John busied himself, writing letters which he would send back to Moose Factory with his former guides and stocking supplies. It was five days before the canoe was repaired and the weather moderated so that he could get away, and by that time he had acquired another Indian assistant. The McTavishes made sure that he was well outfitted, with five pair of moccasins, the most practical footwear for the territory: two of sealskin, two of common caribou, and one of fine caribou. Mrs. McTavish gave him also a pair of beautiful summer moccasins for wearing at home. Again the Company flag was raised for his departure.

After Rupert House the countryside again changed dramatically. He saw limestone hills for the first time, and high, dramatic waterfalls. About eighty miles from Rupert House, his party portaged into Lake Namiskow, where the Hudson's Bay brigades travelling from Rupert House separated, one taking his route to Mistassini, one south-easterly to Waswonapy, and one north-easterly to Nitchequon. This last place was a fifty-day journey from Rupert House and received mail only once a year. A priest, Father Albanel, estimated that Lake Nitchequon was ten days in circuit and Lake Mistassini twenty days. He had never made the circuit himself. John's guide, Namagoons, said that it would take seventeen days to reach Mistassini from Rupert House.

Peter, the newest Indian, was cook for this portion of the trip, and not a very good one, and so John started to make his own bread. As Peter had also lost all their forks, they had to eat with their fingers. One evening John ate a mink that one of the men had shot and cooked for his own dinner and found it quite tasty. Several times they ran into groups of Muskegon, and one evening they camped alongside a party of fifteen, who were catching and drying fish. They exchanged provisions, which was the custom, to the disadvantage of the white man, which was also the custom. John cared for the sick with his pain-killer and exchanged his battered felt hat for a turban made of mosquito netting, which he found much more comfortable.

Approximately half-way between Rupert House and Mistassini, Namagoons cached provisions for his return, pork and flour for five days. They came upon moss-covered rocks with initials carved into them, including those of Donald McTavish and Thomas Vincent from Rupert House, and John inscribed his own beside them. At another point they passed an Indian grave, and one of his men threw a piece of tobacco toward it, for the spirit to use.

This part of the trip was interesting in part because they kept running into small parties of Indians. Also, they caught up to the Mistassini brigade, which had left Rupert House about a week before they arrived there and generally took thirty-five days to make the trip to Mistassini. There were about fifty in the brigade party, thirty men, and women, boys, and children. The brigade had five large canoes for goods, each containing about forty pieces, and each weighing about 90 lb. Each canoe had a crew of six. Five small canoes carried the women and children. The eleven canoes stretched out along the beach, with people gathered around small campfires, was a picturesque sight. Because John expected to reach Mistassini before the brigade, the leader gave him his packet of letters and also some tea, sugar, and flour for Mr. Miller, who was in charge of the post. They left the brigade after breakfast and entered the Namiskow River. That night they camped beside an Indian family who had been setting nets for the brigade. One of the boys gave John a fine duck for supper, and John reciprocated with a little pork.

Three days after meeting the brigade, they entered a bay on Lake Mistassini. For about half a mile the bay was narrow, resembling an avenue in the water, heavily bordered with trees. Soon it became more open, and Namagoons, pointing to a huge boulder on the point of a small island, exclaimed "Mistassini." John took for granted that the lake was named from this stone, which looked like a man's head. Indians regarded it with reverence and looked upon the lake with awe. Some said that it was three days long, others eight days. There was a story told in those parts about a man going to the northern part of the lake and never returning. A search party had gone out and returned unsuccessful many days later, after suffering much hardship. The Indians in this area, although converted to Christianity, still believed in the efficacy of the drum and the power of their conjurers. Even white men had been affected by their beliefs.

So far John had used Bell's map of the route from Michipicoten to James Bay, and he also had brought with him a chart of the North Atlantic and an 1880 map of Quebec, which showed the portion of Lake Mistassini over which he had to pass. He therefore did not make many notes on the lake as he crossed it, which he later regretted. When he began to realize that the lake would be of great interest, he made more careful notes of his route, from which he later made a map.

John estimated the lake to be about 100 miles long, twenty across at its widest, and perhaps 1500 feet above sea level. His map differed slightly from the printed map. He discovered that his observations for latitude corresponded to those on the chart of the North Atlantic for Lake Namiskow. In two places closer to Lake Mistassini approximately fifty miles apart, he found a compass variation of twenty-five degrees, instead of twenty-one as given on the chart. It was only later that he realized the importance of this observation.

It took them another three days to reach the Mistassini Post because the rapids were difficult. The boulders were black and hard to see. They met several parties of Indians, which always meant a visit and exchange of presents. When they arrived at the Post, they were received kindly and spent several days there. John left Namagoons and Peter there, and Miller found two new Indians for the next portion of the trip, to Lake St. John: George as guide and Wiggins as cook. Miller told John to watch for the mile posts that a party of surveyors had put up ten years earlier. The estimated distance was 261 miles.

After John exchanged presents with the Indian chief at the Post and several others who were kind to him, he left with his new guides. The flag was run up, and all the Indians fired their shotguns in a grand salute. Between Lakes Wahquoonuche and Ojebahgoomoo, on a one mile portage, he was amazed to find the needle in his compass turn through 180 degrees. His guide had told him to watch for it, and no doubt had been with Richardson and McQuat, when this local phenomenon had been discovered.

A week later they ran into a party of about twenty Indians, who were very good to them. John received 12 lb. of flour by promising to send back 16 lb. of sugar. The young owner of a drum he had been given earlier was among the group. The boy was upset because his father had given the drum to John without his knowledge. John placated him with a jacknife. In the mean time George attempted to persuade one of the young fellows going to Lake St. John to help him over the portages and show him the way to run the rapids. It appeared that George had never seen that part of the river before.

Early the next day they started out and received the traditional gun salute. The small canoe they were following got away from them in the first set of rapids: not laden with goods, it travelled more quickly. They ran in the worst rapids John had ever seen, sometimes ten miles of unrelieved white water. They ran the last half-mile in less than five minutes! The river was straight, only 100 feet wide, and the spray and foam were so great that it was difficult to see the rocks. They touched rocks twice, and all their belongings were drenched. Afterward George asked if John wanted to kill him, but George now had no choice but to continue. They were now at camp 49, 150 miles from Mistassini and 1,000 miles from Michipicoten.

Several days later they met Charlie Robertson, an old voyageur who spoke English and Cree, and a Mistassini, a free-trader named George, along with their families. They all had an enjoyable camp, dining on fresh bear meat and onions and Wiggins' fresh bread. The free-traders two men from Mistassini arrived on their return trip to Lake St. John and promised, for several pounds of tea, to lead John's party through the next set of rapids. Charlie Robertson told him that the rapids they had just run were the worst he had ever encountered in a small canoe.

The land was very beautiful. High granite hills rose on each side of the river, and the travellers saw several bear but were unable to shoot one. On August 26 they came upon their first clearing, and their next-to-last portage took them through a farm yard. They were down to the last of their provisions and at the farm-house bought bread and a peck of potatoes. Wiggins was fascinated by the horses and carts, the first he had ever seen. That same day they arrived at the Hudson's Bay Post at Pte. Bleue on Lake St. John, where John found his old friend, Mr. Cummins, in charge.

Galbraith had now reached the final stage of his adventure. At Pte. Bleue, he purchased a canoe for $7.00 for Wiggins and George to take back for Miller at Mistassini. His men took some of their pay in goods out of the Company's store and also got their provisions for the return trip. John hired two men for the trip to Chicoutimi and Tadoussac. Farms lined the sides of the river, and several times he hired a Canadien to transport the canoe by cart to its next launching point. When he reached Chicoutimi, he sent a telegram to his brother, Tom, in Tadoussac and asked him to bring fresh clothes. He also hired a photographer to take a picture of camp 57; for four dollars he got three tintypes and two photographs. The photographer was not satisfied with one of the negatives, and took a second.

Winds and tides on the Saguenay River made travel difficult. Rocks stood perpendicular for miles, and there was the constant danger of being caught in a squall, unable to land. After rounding the point at Cape Trinity, they were almost swamped. At another place they were fortunate to find a level spot for the tent on high rock, and they slept tied to the trees with their sashes, which they all found very amusing.

John Galbraith arrived at Tadoussac on September 6. He had left Michipicoten on June 21 and thus completed in seventy-seven days a voyage of 1,200 miles in one canoe.

CHAPTER FIVE

Family Life

WHEN JOHN GALBRAITH RETURNED IN 1878 to live in Toronto and teach at S.P.S., he ran into an old friend from his student days, Frederic Stupart. Frederic introduced John to his sister, Emily. In later years John often told of how he had fallen in love with her when he had seen her on the garden swing as he walked by her home to and from his university classes. She was very young at the time, and her long brown hair blew freely in the breeze, but even then he knew that she was the girl he would marry some day.

They became great friends, and when John was away on his summer camping trips, he took pleasure in writing letters to her, in which he showed the romantic side of his nature. In one such letter he writes:

What do you think of the following? (They are Mrs. Browning's and not mine.) This last remark now that I think of it savours of self conceit on my part and of impertinence to you but I hope you will overlook that as I can't cross it out now.

Say what can I do for thee! Weary thee, grieve thee, lean on thy shoulder – new burdens to add! Weep my tears over thee making thee sad! Oh shun me not, leave me not, let me caress thee, I love thee so, Dear, that I only can bless thee!

Your loving friend, John

John Galbraith and Emily Stupart were married on June 16, 1886, at St. Luke's Anglican Church in Toronto, and for their honeymoon John took her on her first camping trip. He was, by now, a man of forty, who had spent his life working and living with other men in the outdoors. He was a scholar and had been a teacher without the time to think of marriage. Emily was thirteen years younger than he, the daughter of a retired officer in the Royal Navy who had emigrated to Canada in the mid-1830s. The marriage was a good one; she was also able to accept the demands made on his time and his frequent absences from home. She was an excellent homemaker and enjoyed the social life that the University offered.

In December of that same year Emily received a letter from her husband's brother, William, whom she had never met, from Rat Portage, now Kenora, Ontario. He had moved there some time previously and was working for the Hudson's Bay Company. He told her of his impending marriage to May Matheson of Prince Edward Island on Christmas Eve. "The whole town is turning out," he went on, "and May is convinced she will faint." John and Emily did not attend, because Emily was expecting her first child and her doctor thought a long train journey unwise. John's mother and his sister, Jeanie, did go, however, and there Jeanie met a young minister, Alfred Stunden. They fell in love and were married several years later.

John and Emily Galbraith became parents for the first time on April 13, 1887. John sat down that evening to write the news of the birth of their daughter to his mother in Port Hope. But that news came last. He replied to a question she had asked in her last letter. She was curious about the history of the hemlock root he had taken home from his camping trip with his Indian friend, John Peters, ten years before. He wrote several pages telling her the story and also passed on news from his sister, Jeanie – she and her young minister had set the date for their wedding. The last portion of the letter was brief: "You became a grandmother of a granddaughter this morning between 11 and 12. She is according to expert statements a remarkable child, weighs about 10 lbs. – so I must congratulate you. Emily is doing as well as can be expected. Am busy with examinations. Love to Father. Your affectionate son, John." (Telephones in private residences were still a rarity.)

Shortly after Emily Beatrix Galbraith was born, Jeanie, married the Rev. Alfred Stunden. She was radiantly happy, and it was not too long before she became pregnant. However, their happiness was short-lived. Jeanie was an accomplished musician, and as minister's wife she played the organ at church on Sundays. She was waiting in the aisle for her husband after the service one Sunday. William told the story to his father in a letter.

To write to you about the death of our dear Jeanie is almost more than I can bear. The suddeness with which the calamity has come upon us, together with the terrible nature of poor Jeanie's sufferings and death is heartrending. The brave manner in which she bore her severe sufferings together with the tender solicitude shown for the welfare of her dear husband displayed a nature seldom met with.

The accident as you already know by Thomas' letter was caused by the falling of a chandelier immediately behind Jeanie. The chandelier contained six large lamps all of which broke to atoms. Jeanie told me that she felt the lamps strike her dress behind and in an instant she was all in flames. Mr. Stunden was standing immediately facing her and speaking to her at the time. Mr. Stunden instantly drew her to him but in her frantic efforts to get away from the flames she rushed by him and into the vestry. There was only one of the wardens in the church at the time along with Jeanie and Mr. Stunden. The warden immediately ran out and rang the bell to alarm the townspeople. A man passing at the time rushed in and caught Jeanie and had to drag her over the backs of the pews as the aisle was all in flames. I arrived on the scene just as the man had laid her on the passage between the church door and the sidewalk. Her clothes were in such a disordered condition that I did not recognize who it was at first but on getting a look at her face I saw it was our dear Jeanie. I stooped down to pick her up when she exclaimed "Oh Billy isn't this fearful." The thing was all so sudden that they hardly knew what they were doing. I spoke to the warden about running out and leaving Mr. and Mrs. Stunden in the flames and he said he had no time to think but imagining them both to be in flames he said he knew he could not manage the two and therefore tried to get help as quickly as possible. To understand the situation in which Jeanie and Mr. Stunden were placed you must know that there is

43

only one aisle in the church and they could not get out by it on account of the fire being in it. So our dear Jeanie has been sacrificed to the carelessness of an incompetent mechanic who did not know his business as a lamp hanger. The whole thing was hung on a hook screwed into a joist to which was attached a rod and no swivel to allow the thing to turn round. Every time the thing was turned it would naturally loosen the hook in the joist above.

Poor Jeanie was so weak through all her trouble that we could hold very little conversation with her. She struggled hard all last night and passed away quietly this morning about 6.45.

Jeanie was so very happy in her married life that it seems such an awfully cruel ending. She and her husband were thoroughly wrapped up in each other. No couple ever got along more agreeably. She entered into all his works and fully felt the responsibility of her position. Poor Alfred feels her loss keenly and at times is almost beside himself with grief.

Jeanie will be buried on the anniversary of her birth. John and Mother will only arrive that morning.

Jeanie was buried in the Lake of the Woods Cemetery, Rat Portage, Ontario, on May 11, 1888, her thirty-seventh birthday.

CHAPTER SIX

Varsity in the 1890s

B Y ONTARIO ORDER-IN-COUNCIL OF NOVEMBER 6, 1889, the School of Practical Science was reorganized. Galbraith was made Principal, a role he had been fulfilling unofficially for some years. The Principal and a Council of three from the School were in charge of day-to-day operations, under the direct authority of the Minister of Education. Galbraith, as Chairman of this Council, had the delicate position of go-between vis-a-vis the Ministry of Education and the President of the University. Now he, rather than the President, had to report directly to the Minister.

Galbraith's first concern was lack of space in the building. The courses now taught were Civil Engineering (which included Mining Engineering), Mechanical and Electrical Engineering, Architecture, Analytical and Applied Chemistry, and Assaying and Mining Geology. These courses led to a diploma at the end of three years. There was great need for more laboratory space, equipment, and staff. Galbraith approached the Minister to try to arrange for these requirements. The Minister finally agreed that more space was essential if S.P.S. were to function properly and invited Galbraith to accompany him on a visit to some of the better-known U.S. institutions, so that they might have a clearer idea as how to proceed in Toronto. In late 1889 building commenced on an addition, which by late 1890 was ready for occupancy. More than eighty students registered. The members of the Council began discussions on adding another year to the course and establishing a Bachelor's degree in Applied Science. The entrance requirements were too low, in their opinion. French and German, or both, should be added to the curriculum, because students no longer had the time to take these courses at University College.

In February 1890 a disastrous fire destroyed part of University College, including most of the library. Galbraith offered the use of some S.P.S. classrooms to the University after first obtaining permission from the Minister of Education. This annoyed the President, Sir Daniel Wilson, because he felt he should have been the first to be consulted and was the beginning of friction between the University authorities and the Principal. But Galbraith was far too busy to concern himself about the effect that his administration of S.P.S. had on the President. During that year he gave 250 lectures to students in all years, in Dynamics, Strength of Material, Hydraulics, and Thermodynamics. His father died on March 22, close to the end of term, and as he had no replacement he taught all his classes for the day before leaving for Port Hope. His father was buried the following Saturday, and Galbraith was back in the classroom on Monday morning.

One of his innovations – arranging classes from early October only until mid-April – was working well. His students had no trouble getting jobs and were able to put into practice the theories they had studied during the term. They had the opportunity to work with all sorts of men as members of a team and could learn the importance of being observant and accurate in daily written reports. One of his first students, Kennard Thompson, worked as a student engineer for the Canadian Pacific Railway in the Selkirks in British Columbia during the fall of 1885, when the "last spike" of the C.P.R. was driven.

In those years Canadians felt very much a part of the British Empire, and the affairs of the Empire were very important to them. It was not surprising, therefore, that on October 25, 1899, there were no University lectures because of the departure of the South African Contingent from Toronto. There had been enmity for years between the Dutch settlers (Boers or Afrikaners) and foreigners, particularly English. Trouble had arisen over the gold discovered in South Africa. Both factions struggled for control. This finally erupted into war: the Orange Free State and the South African Republic declared war on the British in October 1899.

Canadians were quick to join their British comrades, and everyone went out to see the Volunteers off to fight the Boers. Lectures were cancelled again to celebrate the relief of Ladysmith, near Johannesburg, in early March 1900.

University life was not made up entirely of lectures and examinations. Students had ample free time to enjoy social and athletic activities. Some students participated in the canoe championships held on Lake Ontario; some played football; some were enthusiastic spectators. Principal Galbraith especially enjoyed football and rarely missed an opportunity to cheer on the University of Toronto team. He took delight in the train journey to Kingston with students and faculty to watch Toronto take on Queen's. The trips home were lively, especially when Toronto won. Each faculty had its own yell, and each endeavoured to outdo the others in singing their favourite university songs.

The Annual Meeting of the Engineering Society of Toronto was also important enough to merit cancelling of the odd lecture. It was generally held in late November. One meeting in particularly was notable because of the visit of such eminent professors as Kelvin, Ramsay and Lister of the British Association of Engineers. They came, in part, because of their respect for John Galbraith.

As the number of engineering students increased, so did rivalry between faculties. All united when a Varsity team was playing against another university, but on campus the situation was quite different. Principal Galbraith and the deans of the other faculties spent a great deal of their valuable time on discipline committees. Some fracases were relatively innocent, but some were well-planned, drawn-out battles, and faculty members were forced to intercede to prevent damage to property and injury to students. There were few women attending the University, and no feminine influence to temper high spirits.

It was "Skule", (S.P.S.) against the Medical students, or Medicine and Science against University College. On one occasion men from University College and the engineers had a row that ended with some bright fellow turning on a hose and attacking the others inside the engineering building. Water poured down the corridors, and the professors were furious. Another time, someone fired a

47

shot gun, and a pellet went through a window. Frequently windows were broken by high-spirited students throwing stones or, in winter, snowballs.

Galbraith acted as Chairman of the Discipline Committee and proved a stern but fair judge. He called in the culprits at once and listened carefully to each side of the story. He investigated the situation thoroughly, and more than once discussions continued for several weeks. Those responsible were always punished, but none ever felt that the punishment was unfair; in fact Galbraith was often less harsh than other members of the committee would have liked. It was usually a fine of a few dollars – a lot for a struggling student – often to pay for damages, for example, new glass. Sometimes the punishment was suspension for a few days. Once set, it was not rescinded.

One time Galbraith became aware that a fight was scheduled for the coming Friday. He sent word by messenger to the President and the heads of the other faculties and warned that all students would be identified and punished. The students had their battle on the Friday regardless, and the Discipline Committee met Saturday to determine the punishment. Although Galbraith knew very well who the ring-leaders were, the Committee met each day for the better part of a week to ensure that the punishment was just and fair. Unless there were actual damage and the student wars got completely out of hand, he would walk by with a blind eye.

What Galbraith absolutely did not tolerate was cheating. One Monday morning just after the examination papers had been prepared, the professors discovered that the School had been entered during the weekend. Three of the professors' desks had been opened and examination papers removed and placed in other envelopes. Galbraith's desk had been tampered with but was unopened. Again, no one was expelled, because Galbraith would not act without absolute proof of the identity of the culprits, even though the teaching staff had to spend many extra hours setting new papers.

In one extremely serious situation, the students got into trouble with the City of Toronto. Since 1861 Toronto had had horse-drawn tram cars. The cars had steel wheels and were pulled along a track made of steel rails. In winter, sleighs substituted for cars. At

48

its peak, Toronto had 361 trams and 100 sleighs. One track ran along College Street, which bordered the University grounds. Electric power was introduced in 1880, and by 1892 horse-drawn trams were becoming things of the past. Electric cars ran on a track flush with the pavement and received current through an over-head wire, by means of a trolley. On this particular day a group of students became rambunctious, raced out onto College Street, and pulled down the trolley poles and upset the tram cars. The police were called in, as were the Mayor, and the President of the University, and all the deans of colleges in which the students were enrolled. City officials and the President demanded expulsion, and it was only with great difficulty that Galbraith obtained agreement for a lesser punishment.

CHAPTER SEVEN

Northern Summers

IN 1896 PROFESSOR WILLIAM JAMES LOUDON, was discussing with several of his University friends his idea for a sporting club. He had in mind a piece of beautiful land they all knew about at Rock Lake, between Toronto and Ottawa on the southern border of the Algonquin Park. As Rock Lake was near the headwaters of the Madawaska River, they called the proposed retreat the Madawaska Club. Galbraith was elected one of the directors, with Loudon as general secretary and manager. They decided to offer eighty shares at $25.00 apiece. Some of the men wanted a sporting club only, but others envisioned a spot where they could build cottages and bring their families. Galbraith was one of the latter; the Galbraiths now had three children, Beatrix, born in 1887, Jack, in 1891 and Douglas, in 1893, and he looked forward to a place where he could spend the summer with his family.

Loudon applied for a land grant at the flag station at Rock Lake. It was difficult. The Province was not anxious to grant lands for a summer colony in the vicinity of lumbering activity, because of the danger of fire. Loudon found it easier to obtain permission for a sporting club, and on one of his trips chose cottage sites for himself, Galbraith, and C.H.C. (Charlie) Wright, Professor of Architecture at S.P.S.

At the same time Galbraith was busy preparing for the Annual Meeting of the British Association for the Advancement of Science, which was to be held in Toronto. It was to coincide with the 1897 Diamond Jubilee of Queen Victoria, and many men with world-wide reputations in every field of scientific endeavour would be attending. Social events, such as dinners and teas, were planned, as well as regular meetings. There were lectures designed only for scientists and others open to the general public. Special excursions were arranged, even as far as the west coast. Emily Galbraith was in her element, for she thoroughly enjoyed social affairs and was a gracious hostess.

Loudon came up with the novel suggestion that they take the visitors to see the beauties of Algonquin Park. This area had been set aside by the Government as a National Preserve, both to protect the forests from indiscriminate lumbering and as a preserve for fish and game. He prepared an impressive brochure for the members of the British Association and also a full description of the tour, by rail from Toronto to Penetang, where the visitors would board a steamer to travel to Rose Point, near Parry Sound. There they would board another train to cross through Algonquin Park, then on to Ottawa and Montreal, before returning to Toronto. He added pictures of the Parliamentary Library in Ottawa, a view of Parliament Hill by the well-known Ottawa photographer Topley, and a photo of one of the entrances to Rock Lake. The fare for this excursion was set at nine dollars.

Loudon also suggested stopping at Rock Lake for breakfast. He had an ulterior motive, for he wanted his friends to see at first hand what an ideal spot it was for their proposed sporting club. He assured James Bain, who was in charge of arrangements, that he could put on a breakfast for $200.00. Bain was enthusiastic and offered $250.00, also promising to send along a case of claret, two cases of Scotch, and a box or two of good cigars. James Bain was a Scotsman who knew the needs of the British; Loudon was a teetotaler.

Loudon, Wright, and several others travelled to Rock Lake several days beforehand to set up the breakfast. They erected a large tent, set up tables and chairs, and procured cooking and serving equipment. They used a railway car as their headquarters and hired two of the section men to help. They used some of the liquor as a treat for the men and later said that it was not long

51

before every train both eastbound and westbound was stopping for the crew to have a tot.

The Galbraiths travelled on the train with the more than 200 visitors who made the trip on August 25. As they rounded the point, the large tent with the Union Jack flying was the first sight they saw. The tables were all set up and decorated with wild flowers. Loudon had even made birch-bark containers for extra butter. Their guests feasted on one hundred chickens and on six large hams made up into huge sandwiches. There was also cheese, olives, and fruit, and small cakes of maple sugar were set at every place in tiny birch-bark receptacles as souvenirs.

The day was beautiful: the sun shone in a cloudless sky, birds sang, and the rippling waters of the lake were visible to everyone through the birch trees. The smell of freshly brewed coffee permeated the air. Scientists, their wives, special visitors from the Park, section men, train crew, and black Pullman porters all sat down together. One of the guests, Ramsay MacDonald, was visiting from Scotland on his honeymoon. Years later he became Britain's Prime Minister, and recalled the occasion when he came to Canada in 1929 to accept an honorary degree at the University of Toronto on October 16, 1929. The visitors stayed two hours, long enough to walk about and go out on the lake in the canoes and other boats provided. When the train whistle blew, no one wanted to leave, but already the train was well off schedule.

Galbraith sent Emily along with the others and remained behind for a few days. He and Loudon went off in a canoe to Cache Lake and then to Canoe Lake, to see Mr. Simpson, the Superintendent of the Park; later they paddled into the Tea Lakes and Smoke Lake, which Galbraith had never seen, and he agreed that this area was ideal for the proposed camp.

Unfortunately, this was not to be, and eventually Rock Lake was included in Algonquin Park. All were disappointed that Rock Lake, was unavailable, especially Andrew Fleck of Ottawa, Secretary of the Canada Atlantic Railway, because it meant the loss of good business for his railway.

Loudon came up with a map of Georgian Bay, which contained many small islands. There was some dispute about these, because

Thomas Galbraith, John's father, who came to Montreal at the age of
twelve from Scotland with his parents in 1834

Forge Cottage, 284 Ridout Street, Port Hope: John Galbraith's
home during his school days and later, when he worked in Port Hope.

Jane Anderson Galbraith, John's mother, whose father, John Anderson, came to Montreal from Scotland and married Jane LeBeau, a French-Canadian

Jane (Jean) Anderson Galbraith, John's sister, the only daughter of
Thomas and Jane

John Galbraith with his brothers: William (left) and Thomas (right)

The School of Practical Science (S.P.S.), on University of Toronto
grounds

First University College Natural Science Club, 1867–8

Professor Galbraith in the classroom, about 1900

A basement laboratory; more space and equipment needed!

Jimmy, one of the Indian guides from Michipicoten to Missinaibi,
sketched by Galbraith, 1881

An overnight camp on the 1881 canoe trip

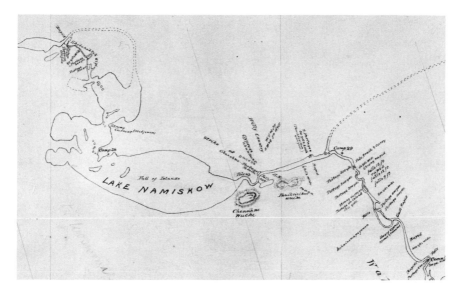

A section of the map drawn by John Galbraith on the canoe trip in 1881

When the wind was right, the Indians used a blanket as a fine sail for a canoe.

Emily Stupart Galbraith,
John's wife

John Galbraith,
Principal of S.P.S., about 1903

Queen's Park: Jack and Douglas Galbraith in the pony cart with Tiny

Emily Beatrix, John and Emily's daughter

John Galbraith in his office at S.P.S.

S.P.S., class of 1907

The collapse of the Quebec Bridge, August 30, 1907: Looking south
from the main pier

The Engineering Dinner, Convocation Hall, 1911

The Galbraith cottage at Go Home Bay. The window from S.P.S. set in the peak gave it "an ecclesiastical air."

John Galbraith in the chair carried especially for him in his latter years

Emily Galbraith feeding her chickens at Go Home Bay

A friend at Go Home Bay standing by the rock where John Galbraith
customarily sat to enjoy the sunset. It is now his memorial stone,
Mount Pleasant Cemetery, Toronto.

Bronze bust sculpted by Emmanuel Hahn and commissioned by John Galbraith's students; it now sits in the foyer of the Galbraith Building, St. George Campus, University of Toronto.

the Dominion Government had juristiction over them and Ontario hoped to establish its authority. Because there was no timber, the group was assured that it could have what it wanted, as long as it agreed to put up cottages. There was a small bay, known as Go Home, were Galbraith had camped on canoe trips. He took Loudon to see it, and Loudon agreed that it would be suitable.

Go Home Bay, is on the Canadian Shield, about twenty miles north of Midland. It is a beautiful spot, with small, rocky islands surrounding both an inner and outer bay, sheltered from the open and rougher waters of Georgian Bay. The name itself is intriguing. "Go Home" was not of Indian origin, but rather thought to have been named by hunters or lumbermen who passed through the bay into the wilds; when they reached it on their return they knew it was "the go home place."

It was 1898 before Government approval was given for the camp at Go Home Bay. In the mean time John visited the spot several times with some of the other prospective members, and he and Charlie Wright picked out their cottage sites, side by side, in the inner bay. It was a decision he never regretted.

Wright and Loudon undertook to start building the Club House, where they all would live while building their own cottages; later the building would serve as a community hall. Galbraith was elected as first president, and Loudon treasurer, to oversee a budget of a mere $500.00. Wright, the architect, designed a long building with a cook-house at one end. Curtains divided the areas, with one end set aside for the women and children, the other for the men. Wright estimated that it would require 10,000 board feet of lumber, at six dollars a thousand. Window frames, complete with glass and paint, could be purchased for three or four dollars apiece.

Loudon turned out to be a master scrounger, and the hall was built within budget. One morning in early spring 1898 Galbraith looked out of his office window at S.P.S. and was astounded to see Loudon, standing beside a wagon and helping the carter load the discarded storm sash from the School that had been stored in the basement. He ran out of the building, demanding to know what was going on. At that very moment Charlie Wright appeared, staggering under the weight of another window, which he almost dropped when he caught sight of Galbraith. Loudon stammered something about going to the Minister of Education, who gave his permission, and apologized for not approaching Galbraith first. The two men stood there looking like small, guilty boys and then suddenly started to laugh. John, unable to trust his own face and still angry, turned heel and marched back into his office, where he watched as they hastily finished the loading and the wagon sped off, with Loudon urging on the driver. The windows served well, and when the Club House was eventually dismantled various cottagers purchased them for one dollar each. John was presented with a beautiful little Gothic window as a peace offering; he installed it in the peak of his house. He told his friends that it gave his place "an ecclesiastical air."

Loudon also managed to get the old bedsteads, tables, chairs, and all kinds of assorted kitchen equipment and utensils from the abandoned residence of University College. While the Club House was not elegantly furnished, it was livable and served while the members built their own cottages. They paid a cook four dollars a week and ate well on the plentiful supply of local fish and small game. When nothing else was available, the cook created a tasty porcupine stew. A favourite dessert was blueberry pie, and the cook's cranberry jelly was very popular.

There were some discomforts, however. Early in the season the blackflies were vicious, and later the summer mosquitoes took their toll. The ladies' long skirts and the mens' old woollen trousers provided some protection. The children, in spite of their bare legs, tolerated the insects better. Leisure clothes were still far in the future, and women did not consider shorts or slacks. Men wore their oldest city trousers with white shirts, adding a suit jacket when necessary, and the women wore light-weight cotton blouses and ankle-length skirts. Large hats protected their heads from the sun. Bathing suits covered their bodies; the men's came down to their knees, and the women added stockings and bathing shoes. No one dreamed of lying in the sun for a tan.

At the end of the summer the camp was closed up for the winter, and a caretaker, who lived nearby, was hired to protect their possessions. During freeze-up, the only way in and out was by dogsled or snowshoes. Many trappers, both white and Indian, passed through. Some travellers used the empty cottage as refuge from storms; others, roving pirates, went up and down the shore removing furniture, even doors and windows, to use or sell. Some cottagers took the precaution of transporting their household possessions to Penetang or Midland for the winter. In an effort to discourage break-ins, the caretaker was paid $15.00 and instructed to build a small cabin on a point and furnish it with two bunks and a stove for the use of stranded travellers.

Within several years, the Galbraiths, along with many other original members, were living in their own cottages, but the Club House was still used as community centre and living quarters.

In 1901 a biological station was started under the auspices of the University of Toronto, the Dominion Government paying for a biologist to study the wildlife at Go Home Bay. The Government was interested in the numerous species of fish, particularly lake bass. Club members were concerned that the traditional Indian method of using nets would, in time, deplete the supply. There was a great assortment of birds, including whipperwills, loons, ducks, hawks, and bald eagles. Turtles, with their young, swimming single-file among the lily pads were a common sight, and there were many species of snakes, such as copperheads, puff adders, moccasins, and rattlers. After dark it was unwise to venture out without shoes: snakes came out to sleep on the rocks which had been warmed by the sun during the day.

Hydrographic and meteorological studies were conducted under the Club's auspices. Eventually the station was transferred to the Department of Marine and Fisheries and closed in 1914. It had served as a valuable training place for young biologists. Experience gained gave direction to the foundation of marine and fresh water laboratories in the University of Toronto.

One summer a man staying at the camp brought a nanny goat and her kid with him and provided fun for all. The goat always knew, intuitively it seemed, when it was time to be milked and invariably disappeared with the kid and hid in some crevice near the water or on the height of land. When the man went home he left Jumbo, the kid, behind at the Club House. Jumbo had a voracious appetite and gobbled down scraps from the table, tit-bits offered by the children, soap, string, and anything cotton, all with equal enthusiasm. John Galbraith once made the mistake of offering Jumbo a piece of his cigar, and from then on the kid haunted the dock, begging from anyone who might spare some tobacco.

Young Jack Galbraith, intrigued by Jumbo, begged his father to let him have the kid at the cottage. All went well for a time. The kid enjoyed himself thoroughly with the children, who fed him well, and John doled out the expected treat of tobacco. Jumbo's life of luxury did not last long, however. One morning John wakened early. He was disturbed by noises coming from the store-house. He discovered Jumbo ransacking the place and arrived just in time to save his precious store of whisky. Jumbo had succeeded in tipping it over and was nibbling on the cork. He was banished on the spot and was so delighted to be back at the Club House that he went on a rampage, devouring everything in sight. That same day he was banished forever, sold to a passing fisherman, who paid for him in fish.

Galbraith spent the remaining summers of his life at Go Home Bay. A friend once asked him if he missed the long canoe trips he was accustomed to take with his Indian friends. On his last trip to the north, shortly before he married, he became the first white man to run the falls and rapids which were then named after him, La Grande Chaudière de Galbraith, on la rivière Ackamonchonan. However, he replied with the story of a group that left on a long trip, ran into bad weather, and was not heard of for a long time; he did not wish to put his family through that sort of anxiety.

At the cottage he was content to sit on the veranda with a book in hand, his dog resting at his feet. In the evenings he watched the sunset from a large rock, deposited by some long-ago storm. From there he could see into the outer bay as he enjoyed his evening cigar. He and Charlie Wright had purchased a forty-foot launch shortly after they finished their cottages and named it the *Madawaska*. They built the triple-expansion engine for it in the S.P.S. laboratories. Emily was upset when the two men left parts of the engine strewn all over the dock and used the children as eager assistants. She preferred to be off down the Bay, visiting with friends, and she was known to spend many a hot evening sitting alone in the launch by the dock, rocking gently in the evening breeze.

Go Home Bay was a social spot. Inhabitants and visitors alike were from the University community and thus had much in common. On Sundays a church service was held at the Club House. It was a colourful occasion. A musician pumped away on a small organ, and on pleasant days the older women, in their long white dresses or skirts and high-necked blouses, with large hats as protection from the sun, sat sedately on chairs. The young people relaxed on the warm rock, their attention distracted by the sound of the birds, a fish jumping in the water close by, or an osprey landing on its nest, high on the top of a tree.

Many Sunday afternoons Galbraith's Ojibwa friends from Christian Island paddled or sailed over. They left their boats lined up on the rock and sat on the veranda enjoying refreshments provided by Emily, visiting and telling stories. It was a special time for the children, who listened wide-eyed to legends of days long gone. Many a warm evening the Galbraith and Wright families might be found sitting in the *Madawaska*, in the middle of the Bay, with friends gathered around in their canoes and rowboats. They would watch the sunset fade and the stars appear and listen to voices that seemed to echo among the rocks, singing all the old favourite songs. After the last notes of *God Save the King* faded away, people reluctantly started home, their lanterns twinkling like fireflies over the dark waters.

CHAPTER EIGHT

A New Era

THE FIRST MONTH OF THE NEW CENTURY – JANUARY 1901 – saw the death of the beloved Queen Victoria, who had reigned since 1837. In the autumn of 1901, the University of Toronto received the new King's son, the Duke of Cornwall and York, and his wife, later King George V and Queen Mary. Days were spent sprucing up the University grounds, and a holiday was declared for the Duke, who was to receive an honorary degree. University Avenue and the Legislative Buildings were alive with colourful flags, and Toronto turned out in all its finery to see the royal couple. The whole University body was assembled as the procession of carriages arrived at the grounds, and everyone was thrilled at the sight of dignitaries and professors dressed in academic robes as they made their slow march into Convocation Hall. The conferring of degrees was an important and solemn occasion. Later a dinner was held in the Legislative Buildings, followed by a reception. The excitement over, staff and students got back to the business of teaching and learning. In honour of that visit, the Ontario Government erected a statue of Queen Victoria in Queen's Park. Not long after their return to England, the royal couple were created Prince and Princess of Wales.

John Galbraith became Principal of S.P.S. in 1889. He carried on all the administrative responsibilities he still had a full teaching load, and now, in 1901 he was asked to draw up plans for a new Mining and Chemical Building to be submitted to Mr. Heakes, the Provincial Architect. During the winter months he worked on the plans and attended many meetings regarding it.

Space was an ever-increasing problem at the School of Practical Science because of larger enrolment. By 1901 even the students were complaining of overcrowding. Seats had been removed from the assembly hall, which was now used as a drafting room. Lighting was poor, ventilation was worse, and library facilities were completely inadequate. The library and reading room together accommodated only twenty students, and there were 226 enrolled. The mechanical and electrical laboratories were in a damp, unheated basement. Bronchitis was a common winter complaint. The Mining Department needed blast furnaces, stamp mills, vanners, hydraulic classifiers, electric separators, models of shafting and tunnelling, and diamond drills. It had one small stamp mill, a vanner, and a small crusher. There were fourteen students to each balance in the chemical lab, and the teaching staff was only half as large as it should be. In order to put extra pressure on the Government, the students wrote and signed a petition to the Lieutenant-Governor-in-Council putting forward their complaints. The petition stated that the future of Ontario depended largely on the successful development of its huge mineral and forest resources, and these should be developed by men trained scientifically, not by the so-called mining experts who ruined many good properties and wasted money. It had always been Galbraith's belief that men were needed to carry out this work, "not with pick and shovel, but with text book, steam engine and dynamo," and he was determined to do his best to make it happen.

Already many Canadian students were going to the United States to study because there was no room for them in the schools here, and they were lost forever to Canada. The petition ended with the following: "The Country needs men. The men are here to study, to fit themselves for the work and have the money to pay for it. All we ask is that the School be strengthened and equipped to meet the work it has to do." This petition influenced the Government's decision to proceed with the new Mining and Chemical Building.

When Galbraith heard that the contract was about to be let for construction, he was most concerned and wrote to the Minister of Education, because the plans showed no provision for ventilation. He pointed out that a building where Engineering and Architec-

59

ture were taught should use the best engineering and architectural technology of the day; ventilation was an engineering problem that demanded special knowledge and experience, and an expert from the Architect's office should be in charge of that part of the work. He considered it impractical to install an efficent system of ventilation after contracts had been let for the walls, floors, and roof and suggested that details of ventilation should be shown on the plans beforehand. The ground was staked out in late March 1904, and excavation began, but Galbraith's concerns had been taken seriously, and in mid-April Heakes informed him that they were to leave for the United States to study various ventilation systems there. The two men travelled to Pittsburgh, Boston, and New York, visiting various places, including the Lying in Hospital of Cornell Medical Center, examining heating and ventilation systems and talking to experts in the field. By the end of April Galbraith was notified that the ventilation system was to proceed according to his wishes.

The years 1900–06 were extremely busy. Staff members were still underpaid, and Galbraith spent much time and energy trying to convince the Minister of Education to raise salaries. Budgets were tight, and it was a constant struggle to keep within the limits imposed by budget committees. The Principal was forever receiving memos that his financial reports were tardy. He made countless trips to the United States, visiting steel works, foundries, blast furnaces, and heating plants, in order to have the most up-to-date technology in the new building and to update his lectures.

Besides designing space and laboratories of S.P.S. Galbraith had also planned the lighting, the arrangement of classrooms, blackboards, and all the other small details. In his travels he always looked for the most efficient set-ups and was therefore intensely interested in a classroom he saw at the Carnegie Technical School in Pittsburgh in 1906. The room was arranged to accommodate only twenty-four students at a time. A class of 120 students was divided into five sections, all taking the same work in the course of a week. The classroom was occupied constantly, from nine to five daily, with an hour's break from twelve to one. For special lectures there was one large room, which seated 200. Galbraith noticed that the desks were copies of his design – an arm chair with a stationary table on the right arm, supported by a single cast-iron leg. While on trips he visited with graduate engineers from S.P.S. and several times entertained them at a "smoker." Often trips were planned to coincide with engineers' meetings, where he was always a much sought-after and welcome speaker.

It was the era of train travel. Electric trams dropped off passengers at the foot of Yonge Street, where they crossed the road, hurrying to catch their train at Union Station, so called because several railways used it. Horse-drawn cabs crowded Front Street, their drivers waiting for customers or letting others off. Soon after 1900, nervous horses were being forced to share the street with automobiles.

Galbraith's children were now older, and so Emily occasionally went on short trips with him. Sometimes he took one of their children. After his father died, his mother went frequently to Toronto by train to spend a few days. His students also went on day excursions by train to visit factories in other centres. There was usually a yearly trip to Niagara Falls to go through the power station there, perhaps a day excursion to Hamilton, and the odd trip to Buffalo. When Galbraith went to the United States, he travelled by the Grand Trunk Railway, leaving from Union Station. His brother, William, and his wife, May, arrived at Union Station by train from Macleod or Prince Albert on their way east to visit William's family in Toronto or his wife's family in Prince Edward Island. Thomas, his other brother, took the train from Weston to Toronto to continue on to visit their mother in Port Hope. Government officials travelled to Ottawa on business; engineers arrived from the United States and other parts of Canada for meetings.

On one weekend tour, in February 1903, he and his companions visited the Pittsburgh Steel foundry at Glassport, and then went on to McKeesport and Dusquesne to see the tube mills and steel works. His group also saw the Jones Houglin Coke plant, the Lowe Processing plant, and the Singer Nimick Crucible Steel Works before going to East Pittsburgh to have lunch and tour the Westinghouse works. He dined at the University Club in Pittsburgh with S.P.S. alumni who lived there, and he presented a portrait to the Club from the University Alumni Association. The following evening, Sunday, he attended the theatre, held an S.P.S. levee for more than thirty, and then caught the 11.30 train for Buffalo. He arrived back in Toronto early Monday morning, in time for lectures and meetings. He always took a berth on an overnight trip, but the trains rumbled and rattled over rough railway beds, not conducive to restful sleep.

Rarely a month went by that Galbraith did not head for the station on his way to Pittsburgh, Portland, Philadelphia, or Montreal, for meetings, to give a speech, to visit a factory, go to a football game, visit his mother in Port Hope, or travel up to Georgian Bay. For a short trip he carried a well-worn club bag with the necessities and took the tram. It was quite different when the family set off for Go Home Bay in July. Then they took two cabs, one loaded down with steamer trunks and bags, the other for the family. They took, along with clothing for two months, flour, sugar, and many other staples required for time spent away from the shopping centres. The family dog always went with them to the cottage – as did the pony.

One Saturday in February, when the Galbraith boys were entering their teens, there was great excitement in the household when a small Shetland pony and cart were delivered. "Tiny" moved into the backyard of the family residence on St. Mary's Street and became the neighbourhood attraction and the bane of Emily's life. It was not long before his young masters taught Tiny to climb the back porch steps, and he sometimes enjoyed a freshly baked apple pie set out on the window ledge to cool for supper. It was frequently Tiny, rather than the family, who had dessert. The boys became a familiar sight in front of S.P.S., waiting in the pony cart to drive their father home after a busy day. It was unthinkable that Tiny should not spend the summer with his family, and so he too travelled by train to Penetang and then by boat to the cottage.

Interspersed in Galbraith's diary of School events in those years were many references to his family and Tiny. His youngest son, Douglas, was the one most accident-prone. It was he who was very ill with measles, who fell and required stitches to sew up a huge gash on his leg, and who overturned the pony cart and broke his shoulder. When these accidents happened, his mother would phone her husband at the University, and he would rush home to take his son to the doctor for stitches or to the hospital for X-rays.

Galbraith's professional achievements were now being recognized. The University of Toronto presented him with a doctorate in 1902, and in 1903 he attended the installation of Principal Gordon at Queen's University, at which he received his second doctorate. He was now relieved of teaching all except fourth-year courses because extra staff had been hired, but his other responsibilities increased in proportion.

In 1889 the Eastman Company had developed a small portable camera that used a flexible roll film. Galbraith purchased one of these cameras and took it with him on his many trips to factories in the United States and Canada; he took pictures to add to his own notes and to illustrate lectures. On returning from such a trip he developed the film onto glass slides, approximately $3\frac{1}{2}$ by 4 inches. All the slides had to be carefully labelled and then stored in small wooden boxes, each of which held 25 slides. He showed the slides to his students in a "lantern lecture." The lantern held a 500-watt bulb and projected a very clear image on a screen. These lantern lectures showed clearly parts of machinery with which he wished his students to be familiar. He also made negatives and developed all the pictures he took when on holiday. This work and also his own research were done after lectures were finished for the day or on a Saturday.

Although he had now been teaching for many years and written out many lectures, he still reviewed these for every class, adding new information and updating them. When a fourth year was added to the School, transforming Engineering into a degree course rather than diploma, the curriculum was completely revised. The Principal had a whole new set of lectures to prepare, again on his odd free evening.

Galbraith clashed frequently with James Loudon, President of the University of Toronto. Indeed, their disputes were symptomatic of a profound dilemma in relations between S.P.S. and the University, resolved finally in 1906. Loudon had taught Mathematics at University College and was involved in the beginning of technical education in Toronto. He worked tirelessly to have the first S.P.S. building established on University property, and he also taught Mathematics in it for a time. He was a grave, reserved man, very different from his nephew, William James Loudon, the University College professor who arranged the breakfast at Rock Lake in 1897. President Loudon had no close friends and no hobbies, except for a love of music. His one enduring passion was the University. He was more a scholar than an administrator, and in any controversial situation he was so firmly convinced that his solution was the correct one that he adamantly refused compromise. It was not surprising that he and Galbraith frequently clashed.

Loudon and Galbraith were both strong minded. Galbraith was as determined to do the best for his School, as Loudon was for his University. Galbraith did not believe that the head of the Physics Department should teach engineering students, and for a long time he had promoted the hiring of a professor solely to instruct engineers. He had asked Louden, who still held the chair of Physics, although he no longer taught, to make such an appointment, but it never happened.

In 1903 Galbraith wished to have the Physics Department at University College transferred to S.P.S., a new laboratory set up, and an instructor hired. Loudon thought such a move ridiculous because University College had a perfectly good laboratory and classes were arranged to accommodate Arts, Medical, and Science students. But Galbraith believed that his students were not receiving the best education possible, and in his report to the Minister of Education he tried to justify the expense, which he considered minimal.

In 1904 George Anderson applied to the Minister of Education for a position as instructor in Physics at S.P.S. The Minister discussed the situation with Galbraith and in a subsequent speech at the University referred to such an appointment. This was the first time that President Loudon had heard of it. He was livid. He immediately fired off letters, to the Minister of Education, demanding that the appointment be rescinded, and to the Premier, reminding him of the amended University Act of 1904 and stating in no uncertain terms that he considered that such appointments should be approved by him. He was intensely annoyed at the Minister's response. Mr. Harcourt regretted that Loudon and Galbraith did not agree about the matter. "In my opinion, Galbraith's work in the School of Practical Science both in regard to the teaching and administration were admirable and I cannot be expected to treat his recommendations lightly." He would "at an early date consult with Principal Galbraith."

Loudon, still furious, was forced to accept the decision and did so with poor grace. A Physics Department became a part of the School. The division of authority had been a sore point with Loudon for years, and this incident was yet another example of how helpless he was in regard to University appointments. In one section of the University Act, S.P.S. was mentioned as an entity separate from the University. By Acts of the Legislature and Orders-in-Council it was controlled and supported by separate votes of money. The University Senate declared in 1900 that S.P.S. should be constituted as the Faculty of Applied Science and Engineering in all matters pertaining to curriculum, examinations, diplomas, and degrees; however, everything else was still the province of the Minister of Education. As a result, the University had under its wing an educational facility over which it had no authority. The Principal of S.P.S. had the added chore of submitting reports, budgets, curriculum, salary scales, and all other administrative matters to both the Minister of Education and the University administration. It was confusing for all parties, and difficult for Galbraith. The Bursar's office was forever sending memos regarding budgets; Galbraith was regularly tardy in this respect, and there were never enough funds to raise salaries for his staff.

The final outcome, after several years of discussion, was the appointment of a Royal Commission on the University of Toronto in 1905, to study the whole relationship of the University and report in particular on "the advisability of the incorporation of the School of Practical Science within the University of Toronto." The result was the University Act, of 1906, which transformed the School of Practical Science into the Faculty of Applied Science and

Engineering of the University of Toronto. The Principal of the School became the Dean of the Faculty, and the way was open for simpler and more efficient administration.

The change was to become official on June 15, 1906. It was on Convocation day during the dinner to the graduating class that Principal Galbraith made the following announcement, reported in the Toronto Star that same evening, June 8, 1906:

A week ago the Senate of the university passed a statute which provides that the School of Practical Science, its teaching staff, examiners, and students, together with the examiners for the degree in applied science and engineering, shall ex-officio constitute the faculty of applied science of the University of Toronto. By this statute the powers of the Senate with reference to the degrees and those of the school with reference to the work of instruction, as also the statute respecting affiliation, remain unaltered. The result is that the university gains, without expense, a fully-equipped faculty of applied science, and in this respect puts itself on an equality with the other great universities of the continent: while on the other hand the school gains public recognition of the fact that its work is of equal rank and dignity with that of the ancient faculties of arts, medicine and law. This action of the Senate forms a fitting close to the history of the school in the nineteenth century.

CHAPTER NINE

Dean and Commissioner

PRINCIPAL GALBRAITH became Dean of the new Faculty of Applied Science and Engineering when it was set up in 1906. As his responsibilities increased, so did his work load. He was in great demand as a speaker and never refused invitations to events connected with either engineering or the University. He was still an examiner for the Dominion Land Surveying and always attended the annual dinners. In that, as well as everything else he did, he researched any new technique, keeping himself completely up to date.

His responsibilities as Dean of the Faculty had first priority, but he was involved with the profession as a whole. For example, at the request of the Minister of Education, he met with a committee of the Canadian Clay Products Manufacturers. It wanted a course in clay working established in the Faculty, and these meetings led to a course in Ceramic Engineering. When prominent engineers visited Toronto, the Provincial Government asked Galbraith to show them engineering sites in which they were interested and to escort them on trips to interesting places like Niagara Falls, with its massive power plant.

He was a distinguished guest at state dinners and Government balls but maintained that if it were not for his wife he certainly would not go dancing. Emily loved these occasions and always appeared looking regal, in satin and lace. These were always great occasions for his daughter and sons, when they grew old enough to attend.

Because the first Engineering Society in Canada had been

formed at S.P.S., a Society Galbraith felt important for the profession as a whole, he took an active part in the Canadian Society of Civil Engineers (C.S.C.E.). For years he was a member of the Executive Committee, and in 1907 he allowed himself to be nominated as President for the upcoming year and was elected. During his career he held many other positions, including the Vice-Presidency of the Ontario Land Surveyors Association, the British Association for the Advancement of Science, and the Engineering Section of the Commercial Association for the Advancement of Science. These positions were not in name only, because he always had a contibution to make.

He had sat on a committee for the original Technical School, reviewing its standards and giving advice regarding the most suitable courses for students. He acted as a consultant for many engineering projects for the Government of Ontario and the City of Toronto, but he never allowed these extras to interfere with his work at the School or the Faculty.

During the years of building and new additions in the Faculty he continued to travel at the request of the Government to investigate heating plants, ventilation, and electrical systems – anything that could make the buildings as up-to-date as possible. When he returned from these trips, he spent hours writing up reports from his notes and incorporating them into his reports and lectures. He carefully filed all his lecture notes at home. They were all written in long hand, and he refused to allow them to be published. He did not contribute to technical literature. His work was described best as that of "a fashioner of tools which have been widely used by other men in the construction of the great engineering works of his time in Canada."

Emily Galbraith kept life comfortable at home. Since the death of his father, his mother spent a lot of time in Toronto. At least once a month she arrived to spend a few days, and her other son, Tom, and his wife, Clara, came from Weston to see her. Frequently Emily went to Port Hope to stay with John's mother, often accompanied by Beatrix. John travelled there on holidays and sometimes stopped overnight on a return trip from Montreal.

Emily's brother, Frederic Stupart, an outstanding meteorologist, had gone to Holland and Switzerland for the best part of a year in 1905. He and his wife had a daughter, the same age as Beatrix Galbraith, and three sons. The Stuparts took their family and Beatrix with them. She and her cousin, Doris, had just finished school, and the year abroad was a wonderful experience for them. They spent most of their time in Switzerland, where they studied music, French, and painting and looked after the younger boys when the Stuparts were out. On their travels they met Stupart relatives in England for the first time, and Galbraith cousins in Scotland.

John Galbraith never visited Europe. Transatlantic travel was by ship in those days, and it took almost three weeks to cross from eastern Canada to Britain. There was no time during the school term for such a trip, and in the summer he preferred to relax in the Canadian wilderness. In 1905 many letters crossed the ocean, because Galbraith wrote to his daughter, often in French, not leaving all the correspondence to his wife. He did the same when his sons started working. In his diaries he frequently mentioned writing to Jack or Douglas.

Within the course of several weeks in the early 1900s Galbraith's diary read as follows: "Monday, Council meeting, estimates; Tuesday, Council meeting 9 p.m.; Wednesday, meeting Canadian Society of Civil Engineers at the King Edward; Thursday, Engineering dinner; Friday, Literary Society dinner, gave address." Rarely a month went by that a trip to Pittsburgh, New York, or some other centre was not scheduled. He attended a dinner at the Hotel Astor in New York and while in that city visited the furnaces and iron works in the new Singer Building. In March 1907 he accepted an invitation to speak at the S.P.S. Club in Pittsburgh. This dinner was held in the private dining-room of the Pennsylvania and Lake Erie Railway Station, and this enabled him to make a quick connection with his train for home. This station has been restored and remains to this day an elegant place to dine. A month later he was back there for the dedication ceremonies of the Carnegie Institute.

He scheduled his research tours for late May, after the students

69

had finished examinations for the year. In 1907 he made an extensive trip, concentrating on types of floors, walls, desks, and locks. He visited a College of Mines in Houghton, Michigan and the Chemical and Geology Buildings in Madison, Wisconsin. He went to the University in Chicago and a high school in near-by Joliet and at all these places took copious notes. He was particularly interested in the set-up of laboratories, noting that the tables in some chemical labs were fitted with gas, water, electricity, compressed air, and vacuum hot water. In Chicago all the large laboratories were outfitted in the same way. He checked the piping and in Joliet noted that the floors slanted toward the drain. The tables he liked the best were made of slate, and many floors were brick. There was no detail too small to escape his attention. In his diary he noted that the keyless locks were not a success at the Rose Polytechnical School in Terre Haute, and mentioned that the plaster walls were crumbling. While in the railway station at Pittsburgh he took time to investigate how fresh air was drawn from the roof, looked at the position of pipes, plates, fans, and conduits, and checked out the air in the lavatories.

He looked at Cornell's chemical laboratory in Ithaca, New York and went to Johns Hopkins, University of Pennsylvania, Columbia, and the Massachusetts Institute of Technology. He noted the names of the companies making the equipment that he considered the best. He visited metallurgy and mining plants. In the Chemistry and Mining Building at McGill University he saw a soapstone table with exhaust hoods. On one trip, which lasted for more than a month, he went to Washington, Baltimore, Philadelphia, New York, Boston, and Cleveland. When he returned he prepared a detailed report.

On this trip, as on every other, he wrote meticulous accounts of the costs, down to the last penny spent. His personal expenses were completely separate from his business commitment. He did not teach this ethical attitude to his students when he discussed the worker's responsibilities to management, because he took it for granted that a man gave a full and honest day's work for his salary. He did tell the students, however, that as their careers advanced and they accepted more demanding positions, they were entitled to ask for a higher salary – they should never underrate their services.

Canadians were shocked to see the headlines on August 30, 1907, proclaiming in large, bold print that the Quebec Bridge had collapsed. It was the largest bridge ever to be built in Canada. The idea was first considered in 1852, when plans were drawn up for a suspension bridge across the St. Lawrence River near Quebec, to carry both railway and vehicle traffic. Years passed before much was done, because traffic did not warrant the expense. However, in 1887 the Quebec Bridge Company was incorporated, and the decision was made to build a cantilever-type bridge near the mouth of the Chaudière River. Theodore Cooper, of New York, the most prominent builder of railway bridges of the day, was hired as consulting engineer. The Phoenix Bridge Company and the Phoenix Iron Company in Phoenixville, Pennsylvania, were selected to manufacture all the materials.

The cornerstone was laid in 1900. Work commenced in 1903. High costs dictated modifications, which the Chief Engineer did not feel would injure the stability of the structure, and by 1907 one of the cantilever arms and a portion of the central girder span were completed. Then a tragedy occurred. An engine driver drove a small locomotive onto the bridge with two loaded trucks of material, and the framework started tilting. Within a minute and a half, according to witnesses, everything crumbled and plunged into the river below. About one hundred men had almost completed their work for the day. Among them were approximately thirty Chaughnawaga Indians, who were unusually adept at climbing and working at the heights that the construction demanded. Eighty-two men lost their lives.

On August 31, a wire arrived at Go Home Bay from Ottawa requesting John Galbraith's presence on a Royal Commission, together with Henry Holgate, C.E., of Montreal, and John G.G. Kerry, C.E., of Campbellford, Ontario, to investigate the cause of the collapse of the Quebec Bridge. The Government recommended that the three Commissioners be paid at the rate of $50.00 a day for days of actual service, with reasonable living and travelling expenses.

Galbraith left immediately for Toronto to see President Falconer at the University. The President approved his acceptance of the appointment, for it would bring considerable prestige to the

University. The following day Galbraith was on the train for Quebec City. En route he wrote a letter to Falconer containing his suggestions regarding appointments to the staff of S.P.S. for the fall term and mailed it from Montreal. By September 4 he was registered in the Château Frontenac Hotel in Quebec City and went to see the site of the collapsed bridge with Holgate.

Their work commenced at once. The first order of business was to rough out a program to examine the wreck in detail. Most of September they spent in Quebec, taking evidence from witnesses, including the injured in the hospital, going over the records of work already completed, and planning the official inquiry. In early September, Emily Galbraith and Holgate's wife arrived to spend a weekend. The two women visited one of the injured Indians in the hospital, and late the following spring Holgate gave Galbraith $50.00 for the Indians.

From then until the beginning of April 1908, the Commission members worked constantly. On Sundays they relaxed, and John took the opportunity to visit his Montreal relatives. Henry Holgate was elected chairman. Kerry and Galbraith travelled to the U.S. factories where the materials were made and took evidence from those in charge.

Galbraith agreed to write all the reports. He spent the next two months travelling, much of the time with Kerry. He was in Quebec City, Montreal, Ottawa, New York, and Phoenixville, Pennsylvania, with an occasional two-day break in Toronto. Unless visiting a site, he spent most of his time closeted in a hotel room, reading evidence, preparing questions for witnesses, writing reports for the Government, and studying documents. In New York he arranged with an American lawyer to take evidence in the United States. He had long conferences with Mr. Cooper, Consulting Engineer on the project, and took time out to dine with Kennard Thompson, his former student and good friend.

Besides visiting the Phoenix Bridge Company in Phoenixville, which had received the contract for the Quebec bridge in 1903 and where the steel was manufactured, Galbraith and Kerry visited other factories that did the same type of work. They went to the Central Iron and Steel Company and the Pennsylvania Iron and Steel Company Bridge Works in Harrisburg, and coke plants and blast furnaces in Philadelphia, and compared the different methods used. They set up tests and experiments and returned several times to make additional checks. In Phoenixville they discussed with the contractor methods of laying out and building up the chords. They examined in detail all the machines used in the manufacture of materials and paid particular attention to how the work was set up in these machines. Galbraith also read as much as possible of the latest scientific material published. He checked to see whether the engineers were keeping abreast of the latest developments.

On December 6, Galbraith left for Toronto, for he never missed the annual S.P.S. dinner. He was back in Montreal on the 8th. The Commissioners took two days off at Christmas to be with their families and returned to work on December 26. New Year's Eve, at midnight, when all the church bells began to chime, John telephoned his family to wish them a "Happy New Year"; then he continued his study on the chord theory. On New Year's Day he did go for dinner at the Kerrys. Then the round of trips began again – Philadelphia, New York, Philadelphia, Phoenixville, and finally back to Montreal.

The Canadian Society of Civil Engineers met in Montreal that year at the end of January, and on January 30 it elected Galbraith President. He accepted an invitation to a state dinner, which he went to Ottawa to attend. The Commission was now in the final phase of its work, and the three men held many meetings to put together the results of their investigations.

Then Galbraith began writing the report. For the next six weeks he spent many hours each day working. In the report itself he set out their conclusions and recommendations, and he put together nineteen appendices, covering every phase of the operation from the conception of the bridge to the final disaster. The published document was 200 pages long. Two other volumes were published, of more than 500 pages each, containing transcripts of each investigation and all correspondence, and a fourth volume contained pictures of each stage of work. John's report was submitted on February 20 and published in the papers on March 10, but it was another month before the appendices were all finished and sent to Holgate for his final signature.

In their conclusions, the Commissioners stated that no one had fully appreciated the magnitude of their work or the insufficiency of available data. Therefore special experimental studies and investigations had not been completed by the engineers at the Phoenix Bridge Company. The professional knowledge concerning action of steel columns under load was not adequate and did not enable engineers to design such structures economically without the use of large amounts of metal. This led to a serious defect in the original design, which was not recognized and therefore not corrected. However, there was no criticism of the professional qualifications of those hired. Further, an experienced bridge engineer had not been appointed as chief engineer onsite, and this failure had resulted in inefficient onsite supervision.

By April 1908 Galbraith was finally back in Toronto, involved in day-to-day University affairs. Space at S.P.S. was again at a premium, and there were plans under way for new buildings. The appendices of the Commission report were not yet finished. Galbraith was busy with the duties of President of the Canadian Society of Civil Engineers and looked forward to a brief holiday at his summer home. In late August he received from Holgate a cheque for a little more than $9,000.00 to cover his services and expenses, and on September 28 he purchased a new house at 57 Prince Arthur Avenue in Toronto's Annex.

Dr. Kennard Thompson of New York at the Engineering Society meeting on December 9, 1914 dedicated to the memory of John Galbraith stated that the report of the Commission was considered "one of the ablest, fairest and most scientific, as well as most humane reports ever written."

While Dean Galbraith was away from Toronto, working on the Quebec Bridge Commission, the graduates and undergraduates of S.P.S. decided to honour their Dean by presenting a portrait of him to the University. The committee in charge selected J.W.L. Forster, an exceptionally fine portrait painter, to do the work. When the Dean returned to S.P.S. in April, he learned to his surprise and chagrin that he was expected to sit for Forster. It was late fall of

1908 before the artist had completed the portrait, which was presented to the University at a ceremony in November.

Staff, students, and graduates assembled in Convocation Hall, and E.W. Stearn, C.E., an early graduate of S.P.S. then living in New York, unveiled the portrait and addressed the audience. He recalled that thirty years had passed since two dozen students had enrolled at the School to study engineering, with the present Dean teaching all the courses. His speech paid eloquent tribute to his former teacher and mentioned that one of the great scientific magazines in the the United States pronounced the report of the Quebec Bridge Commission "the most thorough and able report ever written in any language of a great engineering disaster."

Dr. John Hoskins, Chairman of the Board of Governors, accepted the portrait on behalf of the University. President Falconer jokingly expressed his condolences to the Dean, who was forced to sit there and listen to all the compliments. Falconer said that Galbraith's life's work had been crowned with success and that his monuments could be found in the works of his students throughout Canada and around the world. Many others added their tributes. Then it was the Dean's turn to reply.

As he often did, he departed from his prepared notes. He was not one to take all the credit and referred to Professor Loudon, later President of the University, for having done more than anyone else to bring about the teaching of applied science and being the first to recognize a need for practical demonstrations. Galbraith recalled that, as a student, he had received a double first in Chemistry without ever having poured an acid into a test tube. The number of students and faculty in 1908 meant that no one was getting the opportunity he had had to get to know others well. "They were getting a different education and not necessarily a better one. I am glad you like the portrait," Galbraith continued. "I certainly liked the artist. I have never had my portrait painted before and it is very different from having your picture taken. I got so that I enjoyed the sittings; it is a really pleasant way to pass the time."

As he spoke, he walked back and forth, speaking in the informal manner his listeners loved. He gave credit to other professors who through the years had contributed so much to the development of the "Little Red School House". Today the portrait presented that day hangs in the Council Chamber of the Galbraith Building at the University of Toronto.

CHAPTER TEN

Toronto and Go Home Bay

THE ACADEMIC YEAR FOR STUDENTS finished toward the last week of April, but not for staff. There were still examination papers to mark, building and laboratory conditions to assess, budgets and curriculum to set up, and many other administrative duties. It was not until late June that John Galbraith was able to think of his own holiday, and it was always a delight for him to take the train north in early July, to catch the boat to his summer place at Go Home Bay. It was there that he relaxed completely and gathered his energies for the next academic year. It was there that he indulged in his other lifelong love, literature, reviewed his lectures for the following term, and studied up on subjects with which he felt his students should be familiar. He never taught anything he did not fully understand himself.

It was at Go Home Bay that the Galbraiths entertained their friends. Emily delighted in it. Every year she made her special dessert of Snow Pudding for Charlie Wright's birthday; it was her specialty in Toronto on Christmas Day. She took pleasure in seeing the girls in their cool blouses and skirts, short enough to show their ankles, and also took pride in her own appearance. For dress occasions the young men wore white ducks, which they rolled to their knees when they went on picnics, so that they could carry the girls from the boats to dry rock. An evening often ended with a singsong around a bonfire and the national anthem.

James Bain, Chief Librarian of Toronto, was a frequent visitor. He and Galbraith were close friends: both were widely read and liked nothing better than to sit long into the evening discussing a good book. He was visiting in August 1900, the year that the first Regatta was held and took an enthusiastic part in preparations.

For weeks before the Regatta the young people practised. They paddled, they rowed, and they swam, to be ready for the upcoming events. The girls helped their mothers bake cakes and cookies. They made dozens of sandwiches. In the ice-house they scraped sawdust off the large blocks of ice for large jugs of lemonade. The men used bunting and flags to decorate the Club House and the Galbraith and Wright cottages, where the events were to take place.

On the day of the first races, excitement ran high. The members of the Club and their guests gathered for the rowing and canoe races. Emily received some of the adults on her veranda, while others watched from the Wrights'. The young people sat about on the rocks, prepared to cheer on the contestants, and the small children ran about, chasing each other and getting in everyone's way. Indians from nearby Christian Island arrived to join in the fun, and their boat races were the noisiest and funniest of all.

Afterward the young ladies served refreshments to their friends on the veranda and the Indians on the rocks. Emily, as the wife of the President, had the honour of presenting the prizes to the winners. Later on the Galbraiths' dining room and veranda were cleared, and one of the men played the violin for dancing. Several days later the swimming and dinghy races were held, and all assembled in the Club House, where, again, Emily presented the prizes. The winning girls received silver spoons, boys fishing tackle or paddles, and flags were presented for the dinghy races. No one was forgotten, because all participants got boxes of candy. After such a summer John Galbraith, his family, and the other cottagers returned to the city relaxed, rested, and ready for the tasks ahead.

In Toronto, John would plunge back into his routine. He was a familiar figure to all the students at S.P.S. He was noticeable in the corridors. He knew everyone by name, and his students were comfortable stopping him to ask advice or merely to chat. Probably one of the reasons he was so approachable was his appearance. He generally looked somewhat rumpled, which was certainly no fault of his wife. She was sure he was colour-blind: unless she laid out his suit, shirt, and tie for him daily, he was apt to escape in brown trousers and a blue jacket. She worked hard to make sure that he did not disgrace either her or the School. After their telephone was installed, she was even known to phone the janitor and ask him to peek into the classroom to see if Dr. Galbraith looked alright, because he was blissfully unaware of what he was wearing. It was his very ordinary appearance that endeared him to his students.

Social life in Toronto was very different from that at Go Home Bay. John left early in the morning for a round of teaching, meetings, and often dinners, from which he might not return until well after midnight. If he were home for the family dinner, he disappeared immediately afterward to work on his lectures or a speech or to study and read. Emily looked after the house and the children. She reserved one afternoon a week for visiting. She set out impeccably dressed, wearing a large hat and gloves, and carrying her silver case with her engraved calling cards, to have tea with her friends. One afternoon each month she received at home, and guests dropped their cards into the small silver dish on the table in the front hall.

Many of the dinners her husband attended were for men only, but at many others she sat at his side, a dignified lady, elegantly though not expensively dressed. She looked forward to the annual ball at Government House and the large affair at the Royal Canadian Yacht Club. Her father, Captain Robert Douglas Stupart, had been instrumental in its inception, and she often took the ferry to the nearby island to enjoy afternoon tea with friends on a pleasant day.

John devoted himself to his work on the weekdays, but never allowed anything to interfere with Sunday, which was sacred to the family. As a Presbyterian, he had been brought up to respect the Sabbath, and Emily was a devote Anglican. Sunday was a day of rest. In the morning they attended St. Luke's Anglican church, where their daughter and sons sang in the choir. When they moved to Prince Arthur Avenue they went to the Church of the Redeemer which was within walking distance and Beatrix continued to sing in the choir. Afterward they returned home to roast beef, Yorkshire pudding, mashed potatoes, and canned peas, followed by ice-cream, a weekly treat. The ice-cream was made at home and placed in a metal container that sat in a wooden bucket filled with ice and covered with salt. When the boys were old enough, it was their chore to turn the handle until the mixture froze.

Later on Sunday afternoon, if they were at home, Emily served high tea, a custom of her English ancestry. Rolled watercress and asparagus sandwiches, dainty egg sandwiches, and hot buttered crumpets were set out on the tea-table in the parlour. A silver-handled knife lay beside the large Royal Doulton cake plate, ready to cut the two layer cake, covered with chocolate icing topped with nuts or with white icing sprinkled with coconut. Emily poured from the large silver tea pot for friends and relatives who dropped in; Beatrix passed refreshments and refilled plates with the help of her young friends. Young people and children loved to accompany their parents to the Galbraith home, because John was a genial host and entertained children and adults alike with his stories. Other Sundays it was their turn to visit, and they would set off as a family to make their calls.

John Galbraith was a contented man. He did the work he enjoyed, he lived in a happy household with a family he loved, and he spent the hot summer days at his beloved Go Home Bay. He desired nothing more.

CHAPTER ELEVEN

Conserving Canada's Resources

THE LAST DAYS OF 1908 AND THE FIRST OF 1909 were busy and difficult. John's mother had hit her head badly in a fall during the previous summer and had never completely recovered. On New Year's Eve, when John was in Port Hope for a short visit, she had a stroke. His wife arrived on the 4.12 p.m. train from Toronto on New Year's Day, his brother, Tom, shortly after. By January 4 she seemed no worse, and so John returned to Toronto, leaving Emily and his brother and wife, who had also arrived, to care for her. The next few weeks were hectic. John had to go to Montreal for meetings, his brother, William, arrived after a train journey of four days from Fort Macleod, where he was manager of the Hudson's Bay Company Post. Emily travelled back and forth from Port Hope, and John went there as often as possible. He still had his lectures to give, and there were numerous planning meetings at the beginning of each term.

At the same time the Engineering Society of the Faculty of Applied Science was preparing for the annual meeting and was expecting 200 members of the Canadian Society of Civil Engineers (C.S.C.E.) to attend. Galbraith was the retiring president of this latter group and, as such, was expected to give the address at its annual meeting also being held in Toronto.

The opening session of the Engineering Society was held on Wednesday, January 13, and the following Tuesday John's mother died. William had remained with her constantly, as had Tom's wife, Clara, while Emily and Tom commuted back and forth. The funeral was held at her home on January 21, with Professors Ellis and Wright of S.P.S. attending, along with many townspeople. Her sons were impressed with her organization; all they had to do was follow the instructions she had written in detail. Unfortunately for her descendants, her sons destroyed all of her personal letters, carefully bundled together in consecutive order, according to her wishes.

A week later, on the morning of January 28, the C.S.C.E. held its first meeting at the King Edward Hotel in Toronto. This was followed by a reception at Government House, and that evening Galbraith delivered his valedictory address as retiring President.

He began by telling his audience that he had jotted down ideas as they had occurred to him and then had had a problem putting it all together. He entitled the talk "The Engineer and His Work" and spoke from the point of view of the engineering teacher, not the practical man in the field. He traced the history of the engineer back to the early Greeks and Romans, using two words, "unxavin" and "ingenium." The root idea of the first meant contrivance, resource, ways and means: of the latter, nature, intelligence, ingenuity. The phrase "mechanical genius" described the highest attribute of the engineer, the control of mind over matter. The remains of the structures of ancient civilizations demonstrated the abilities of men skilled in surveying, levelling, drawing, hydraulics, excavation, and construction. He told the story of a hydraulic engineer of Rome's Third Legion, by the name of Nonius Datus. Datus had been sent to the township of Saldae in Mauritania on the coast of Africa, – known today as Bejäia (Bougie), Algeria, – to investigate why two sections of a tunnel did not meet in the middle. On his way he had been attacked by brigands, who robbed him and injured him, but after resting he carefully took levels of the mountain, drew plans, talked to the contractor and workmen, and went away satisfied that all would be well. Four years later he was called back. The workmen from each side had again diverged slightly to the right, and so they were in danger of having two tunnels instead of one. Nonius solved the problem by having a transverse tunnel constructed to join the two arms, and there was great rejoicing when the waters of the Ain-seur finally arrived at Saldae. John remarked that Nonius Datus was perfectly well qualified to be a member of the Canadian Society of Civil Engineers; the only difference between him and other members was his fluency in Latin. He discussed how "the Romans as a rule constructed their aqueducts with grades approaching those of our modern railways. They tunnelled mountains and bridged valleys, not it must be remembered that they were ignorant of the fact that water could be carried across valleys in inverted siphons but because they were unacquainted with the use of cast iron. There is at least one instance of a masonry or perhaps a concrete pipe constructed by the Romans which was able to withstand pressures as high as ten atmospheres."

He went on to talk of the invention of gunpowder, the introduction of iron, the use of coke, and finally the invention of the steam-engine, by James Watt. To illustrate the genius of Watt, he told the story of Sir Walter Scott and Watt meeting when Watt was 82 years old. Scott described Watt as not only a great mechanical engineer but also an expert surveyor and civil engineer, a philosopher, and a chemist. Watt spoke knowledgeably on every subject that was introduced.

Galbraith analysed the functions of the engineer as follows:

1. Design – the preparation of the drawings, specifications and estimates of cost for works not yet in existence – the study of the problem, the devising of ways and means – in short, the consideration of all questions affecting the construction and efficiency of the contemplated work.
2. Survey and inspection – making the examination of existing works or ground for the purpose of determining necessary extensions and changes – laying out new work – measuring work done – inspection of materials and workmanship, and generally the superintendence of construction.
3. Superintendence of the operation and maintenance of works in running condition.
4. Determining and estimating costs of various kinds.
5. Reporting upon various physical and financial features of existing or proposed works.

To be successful the engineer must have knowledge, training, experience, judgement, resourcefulness, business capacity and ability to deal with men, in fact the qualifications which are necessary for success in any line of work.

He spoke at length on this topic, emphasizing that an engineer must be an educated man in the best sense of the word but did not have to be an expert geologist, mathematician, chemist, lawyer, accountant or any other profession – only engineer. He should know the limitations of his own profession and therefore have some knowledge of surrounding fields. Galbraith's premise was that engineering education should deal more with non-engineering subjects, for the time for training was short and engineering life long. One of the most important subjects was English, because the engineer should be able to think clearly and express himself concisely and in understandable terms. He should also be knowledgeable in business matters, for he must understand costs of materials and be competent to read a financial statement.

Galbraith continued,

The practical sciences are taught in the engineering schools and are applied by the engineer in his work. The teachers of practical science should keep in touch with the requirements of engineers and manufacturers and not develop merely into laboratory investigators following their own lines of thought, indifferent to where these may lead ... . The schools should devote their energies to the teaching of principles. The teaching of practical methods should be chiefly for the purpose of making the connection between theory and practice, thus clarifying and impressing the principles on the student's mind.

He felt that a student should be able to understand a legal contract and should be taught business methods. He foresaw a time when businessmen would attend universities to study business administration. At the time they were as prejudiced against academic training as the practising engineers had once been.

One of the dangers Galbraith envisioned was that of an engineer specializing and then graduating and not being able to find a job in his field. He felt that courses should be designed to be common more or less to all branches, so that a properly educated engineer could adapt himself to new situations. In his view a broad education was the best preparation for later specialization. It was not enough to learn of materials through books. A student should know the history, sources, methods of manufacture, and every other detail. An engineer should not examine the finished product only but watch the whole process of every type of material going into the project, from beginning to end. He should know not only the cost of the work done under his supervision but also the cost to the proprietor and the contractor. He should keep in touch with the labour market and have a keen interest in the physical and social welfare of the men doing the work. In short, the engineer must be many-sided, thoroughly acquainted with his own part of a job and able to co-operate with others.

Galbraith went into the history of the word "civil" as it pertained to the engineer. At one time it was used to denote the difference between one engaged in military works and one building bridges, roads, railways, canals, and similar, civil projects for the general public. He suggested that the engineering profession in Canada should be represented by a single, authoritative body, similar to the Medical Council or the Benchers of the Law Society. This body should oversee qualifications for professional standing, ethics, and all other subjects of professional interest, in order to strengthen its relationship with the public.

In conclusion, he talked of the pride that Canadians should have in their country and of their responsibilty to conserve its resources:

The mines are our treasure houses, which once emptied can never again be filled, while the scattered gold, silver, copper and iron that remain in the country may to some extent be recovered after having fulfilled their first uses, the coal, oil, and gas once used are gone forever. The preservation of our fisheries and forests demands our first attention. Their cultivation must begin and their mining must cease if we are not to lose them altogether.

There would be new problems, he added, which would stimulate research and invention. All the skills and knowledge of the engineer would be required in developing hydroelectric power and ensuring wise use of natural resources. He pictured the day when the automobile would displace electric transportation in the cities. People would travel in underground tunnels and enjoy air

85

travel for pleasure. After thanking the members of the Society for their attention he sat down, to resounding applause.

Following his speech, the guests moved into the Convocation Hall drafting room, which had been transformed into a banquet hall, to join the members of the University's Engineering Society at their annual dinner. Long tables were set up, covered with spotless white linen tablecloths and decorated with vases of flowers. On one wall was a large shield of welcome to the C.S.C.E., draped with flags, and, on the wall opposite, the portrait of Dean Galbraith, also draped in bunting and flags. More than 800, including students, sat down to eat at 9 p.m., with overflow forced to sit on the floor in the corridor outside. The School yell, the "Toike Oike," resounded through the room. The hungry men ate and enjoyed a singsong, and then the after-dinner speeches began.

After the toasts to the King and Canada, A.D. LePan introduced Byron E. Walker as "a man who fingers with a touch, perhaps the most sensitive in Canada today, the throbbing pulse of Canadian life and conditions." In reply Walker spoke directly to the students about their responsibilty to future generations of Canadians. He spoke also of the danger of not conserving the wealth of the country. He talked of a country of only 7.5 million people, possessing great resources, and the large country to the south, exhausting its. President Falconer was received warmly when he rose to speak. He urged his listeners to "bear in mind the advice they had received from Dean Galbraith, that the importance of the man has to be considered as well as that of the engineer and that self control is absolutely necessary."

The Engineering Society's dinner had been intended as a personal tribute to Galbraith and Dr. Ellis, two of its charter members, and the Dean was delighted to have both his brothers and his two sons share the evening with him. The climax was a presentation, by the first graduate of S.P.S., Mr. J.L. Morris, on behalf of the graduates, of a chest of sterling silver flatware to the Dean and a gold watch and chain to Dr. Ellis. It was 1.30 in the morning before the guests left.

The busy week continued. The following day the engineers went on an excursion to Hamilton and Port Colborne, returning to

Toronto by train in the evening, just in time for the annual dinner of the C.S.C.E. at the King Edward Hotel. Meetings continued all through Saturday. Sunday, John was off early to Port Hope, and by Wednesday he was back in his office as usual, he and Tom having disposed of his mother's possessions and settled all the accounts.

CHAPTER TWELVE

Full Circle

OVER THE YEARS FACULTY MEMBERS, particularly John Galbraith, had spent many hours reviewing and revising the curriculum. Up until 1892, when a fourth year was added to the Engineering program, a graduating student got a diploma, but by 1906, when S.P.S. became the Faculty of Applied Science and Engineering, a graduate received a Bachelor of Applied Science, B.A.Sc. In order to upgrade entrance requirements, Galbraith had also, at the request of the Minister of Education, acted as a consultant on revising high school matriculation standards. He had always maintained that, besides Mathematics and Sciences, languages, especially English, and business methods were also important. The definition of an engineer was "a man who does things," and before Galbraith's time an engineer was taught "how to do things." Galbraith endeavoured to teach his students "to know why." Besides the financial and academic reasons for arranging courses over an eight-month period, he recognized that the students' minds required a rest from receiving ideas and needed time to put ideas into practice. He knew from his own experience how satisfying it was to return to class in the fall after time spent in a totally different environment.

Many graduate engineers from S.P.S. were now working throughout Canada and the United States. Some had applied to become associate members of the Institution of Civil Engineers (I.C.E.) in London, England, and had been refused admission. England was still very much the Mother Country, and engineers desired a closer connection in their professional lives. This led to a series of letters in 1907 between Maurice Hutton, President of the University, and J.H.T. Tudsbery of the I.C.E. President Hutton wrote (March 6) of his hope that there could be a "closer affiliation of this new but already great University to the Universities and Learned Bodies of Great Britain and Ireland." Apparently one very important letter had gone astray several years previously, and when Tudsbery and another professor from England visited Toronto a year later, they were at cross-purposes with Hutton. The Englishmen who knew about their letter, supposed that nothing more needed to be said, and the University presumed its had been received and wondered why it had not been answered. The misunderstanding concerned high school matriculation; it was eventually cleared up by the President, opening the way to graduates of S.P.S. joining the I.C.E. This matter had been of great concern to Galbraith, and he was delighted to see it finally resolved.

The Dean was one of the men asked to entertain Andrew Carnegie and his wife on their visit to Toronto in the spring of 1908. He attended the Building Exchange Dinner and presided at a lecture on the new "flying machines." Several days later he gave the address at the Cement and Concrete Exhibition. He went to the dinner at the Cement Association in Toronto and then travelled to Cleveland, to be present at a dinner for S.P.S. men. While in Cleveland he visited the rolling mills and gave a lantern lecture on the Quebec Bridge disaster. The rooms in the Engineering Club were too small to hold the 160 who attended. Before going home he spent some time at the Bethlehem Steel Works. His notes of these trips were incorporated into his lectures and into reports for updating and improving the S.P.S. buildings themselves.

Galbraith was one of a group of professors concerned with industrial education, and in October 1910 he was called upon to act as consultant for technical education in Ontario and to sit on a Royal Commission to set up standards. It was his report that was finally adopted. In October he also went to Berlin (later Kitchener), Ontario, for the inauguration of the Niagara Power Transmission, signed the last of the old S.P.S. diplomas up to and including 1906, attended a dinner at Government House, and went to Cobalt, to advise on a problem there.

In 1911 he was invited to Winnipeg for the meeting of the

C.S.C.E. Before he accepted, he asked permission of President Falconer and suggested that W.H. Ellis act as Dean in his absence. Emily travelled with him, and the highlight, as far as she was concerned, was lunch with the mayor. Shortly after that he was presented to the Governor General, the Duke of Connaught, who was at the University of Toronto to receive an honorary doctorate, and attended the reception. This was all on top of the everyday routine of administration and lectures. It is not surprising that this schedule was beginning to take its toll, and on December 8 he missed his first Senate meeting. While in Montreal in January 1912 to attend the C.S.C.E. meeting, he did not go – for the first time – on the excursions with the other engineers.

John Galbraith was now in his mid-sixties, and in his daily diary he more frequently mentioned days spent in bed. He would get up and go to work, then spend the next several days in bed, and finally a new pattern evolved. On Friday he lectured, attended Council meetings, a dinner, and a Senate meeting, and then went home to bed. He stayed there for the weekend and, unless there was a meeting, Monday morning. Then, determined to carry on as usual, he was up and off to give a lecture, go to a meeting, or attend a dinner, often as guest speaker. Sometimes he was forced at the last minute to ask a colleague to give a lecture for him, as he was too ill to leave his bed.

His wife and family worried, but Galbraith was not a man to disappoint those who counted on him. In order to attend the Annual School Dinner he remained in bed for hours before, and the day after. He missed the Class of 1907 dinner, which was as much of a disappointment to those who attended as to Galbraith.

Galbraith continued to accept requests to act as a consultant, for he believed that part of his responsibility as an engineer was to give his expertise when required. In April of that same year a committee was formed to standardize matriculation requirements for admission to the various engineering faculties in the Province. Galbraith had previously been involved in this area and had definite ideas on the subject. A representative from Hamilton and from McGill and three men from Queen's, joined the President of the University of Toronto and four representatives from S.P.S. on the committee. In September 1912, Galbraith was also called into consultation with the Deputy Provincial Secretary to amend the name of the Association of Plumbers and Steamfitters to that of the Ontario Society of Domestic Sanitary and Heating Equipment.

After the New Year in 1913, he did not make many trips outside Toronto, one exception being a banquet in his honour in Ottawa. His only social events were family affairs or connected with the University. At the end of January Galbraith was called in as a consultant to examine the filters and pure water reservoir at Toronto Island. He examined the Pumping Station and visited the plant. A good portion of his report on this was written in bed. The Bursar at S.P.S. sent him one of his periodical memos asking for advice on the most economical type of coke to use in heating the University buildings.

He attended dinners in Toronto and elsewhere, where often he was the guest speaker. He worked on a problem with the bridge across the Saugeen River at Southampton, Ontario, and in his report he pointed out the importance of an engineer's having full powers of inspection and rejection granted in his contract. He was asked to go to Cobalt to examine mills and to New York for a dinner. He travelled to Nipissing and Haileybury to attend a large dinner and examine the site of an accident. The President of the University regularly gave his permission for these trips: through Galbraith, the University as a whole was being recognized.

The Engineering course at Toronto was becoming well known throughout the world, and there were inquiries from as far away as Russia. When the Toronto Harbour Commissioners prepared a short brochure for a visit from delegates to the June 1912 International Congress of Navigation, they observed: "Toronto is the seat of learning for Canada, an average of eight thousand adult students being in attendance every year at her various colleges and universities, the chief of which is the University of Toronto in connection with which is one of the best equipped faculties of science in the world."

On March 7, 1913, Galbraith noted in his diary that Pauline Johnson – Tekahionwake – had died in Vancouver after spending a year in hospital suffering from consumption. Her father was a Mohawk Chief and her mother, an Englishwoman. She herself was a gifted writer, a poet, whose books were prized by the Dean. Over the years he had maintained his close friendships with many Indians, and more than one tribe had honoured him by making him a chief. They loved him because of his interest in their customs and his efforts to converse with them in their own languages. They respected him for his knowledge of woodlore. One of the Indian names for him was translated as "The Little Chap with the Sunshine Face." An Ojibwa chief, Peter Jacobs, who had once visited Queen Victoria, was a special friend, as was John Peters, whom he had known since the days of the Foley Survey in 1866. One evening Peters and Galbraith happened to camp alongside Jacob's encampment. While sitting around the campfire, under a canopy of stars, the Indians decided to make him an honorary chief. They named him Nawaquekijig (Noonday Sun) and presented him with a magnificent feathered headdress, of which he was very proud. Later, the Cree made him a chief of their tribe, calling him Apitatchesekan, or Half-Day.

In his diary Galbraith notes his first automobile ride, around the city at the end of June; the following day he was in Ottawa, attending a state dinner. Later in June he had a series of doctors' appointments, which confirmed a serious heart condition. The doctors advised him to rest, and so Galbraith left for his annual retreat at Go Home Bay, where he enjoyed a quiet summer resting, relaxing, and restoring his energy. He puttered on his boat engine, chatted with his University and Indian friends on the veranda of his cottage, and spent hours around the bonfire, telling wide-eyed children tales of Indians and fairies. Again he returned to his School ready to tackle the year ahead.

The year 1913 saw several important anniversaries at S.P.S. Fifty years earlier, in 1863, John Galbraith had entered University College, determined to be an engineer. Thirty-five years earlier, in 1878, the School of Practical Science was founded and the Engineering Society of the University of Toronto was established in 1885, the first professional Society in Canada.

The Society's anniversary dinner was held in the large drafting room of the Little Red School House on 5 December. Alumni congregated in Toronto, and downtown hotels were full, as groups of friends met to reminisce. They came from as far away as

Vancouver, Moose Jaw, and Winnipeg. Graduates arrived from Ottawa, and Montreal sent a delegation of sixteen. Kennard Thompson, who had conceived the idea of an Engineering Society, and now worked in New York, left important meetings in New Orleans and missed a Senate meeting in Washington to be present. Engineers from Pittsburgh, New York, Madison, Cleveland, Buffalo, and Denver were there. Former students arrived from north, south, east, and west. They came with one purpose in mind, to pay tribute to their Dean.

Before the dinner, some of the original members of the Society gathered in the Engineering Building, where they re-enacted an old-time meeting, with their first President, John Galbraith, in the chair. At 8 o'clock, when all the guests were assembled in the banquet hall, the Dean, accompanied by G.I. Morris, class of 1881, the first graduate, and G.H. Duggan, class of 1883, arrived. As the Dean paused at the door, 600 white handkerchiefs appeared from 600 pockets, and 600 voices broke into cheer after cheer as the grand old man, who had merited and won the deepest affection of those assembled, proceeded to the head table to take the place of honour.

The undergraduates sat, awed, among the country's most eminent engineers. They knew the Dean. He was the man they met in the hallways of "Skule." He was the man who stopped to chat, called them by name, and inquired as to their progress, the man who accompanied them to athletic events and enthusiastically supported their team. He could be stern, they knew, but punishment, if meted out, was always fair. He was a man with whom students felt comfortable; his door was always open when they had problems, and they knew that they would receive good advice. They were overwhelmed by this group of respected engineers who were cheering their Dean.

The dinner was the greatest ever held by any organization at the University of Toronto, and the evening was a tremendous success. The "Toikeoikestra" played, singers entertained, and speaker after speaker stood up to honour the Dean, their beloved "Johnnie Galbraith," one of the most respected men in the profession. They spoke of his achievements within the University community and outside, but mostly they spoke of their deep respect and their love.

"The debt we owe to our Dean cannot be measured. He has taught us to be men as well as engineers." Telegrams were read from those unable to attend, from Cobalt, from Colorado, from New Jersey, and from Saskatoon; for the Dean," said one speaker, "was not merely the Dean of engineering in the University of Toronto, but the Dean of the engineering profession in Canada. There was no country in the world that had not men who would fain be there, that they might drink to the health of Dr. Galbraith, their science father."

As the Dean rose to respond, the room resounded with cheers and an enthusiastic "Toike-oike" from the students and then became silent. For once he was at a loss for words, touched to the heart at the tremendous tribute. He said, "Thank you," and then without a written speech or notes began to talk to "his boys." He told of the early days, the difficulties encountered, and the development of the Faculty, interspersed liberally with anecdotes. He remembered student after student, where they had gone and what they were doing.

The undergraduates sat listening, enthralled, watching elderly men hanging onto every word their Dean had to say. When he sat down, every man rose to his feet and cheered. The dinner broke up at 1.30 in the morning, and the students left with the engineers – men now, part of the fraternity of the engineering profession.

The following day Dean and Mrs. Galbraith held a reception for the alumni in the Engineering Building. The room was beautifully decorated with bunting and flags. Decorating the table was a large wicker basket full of American Beauty roses, which the students had presented to the Dean for his wife the evening before. Dr. and Mrs. Galbraith and their daughter, Beatrix, received the more than 500 who attended. Mrs. Galbraith wore a black satin gown with lace to match and a black hat with a white plume. Her daughter was dressed in golden satin, with a black hat, and carried a yellow chrysanthemum bouquet. The daughters of their friends assisted in the tea room, and the "Toikeoikestra" played during the afternoon for dancing.

The past year had been eventful. Beatrix started to work in the Bank of Commerce, and Jack graduated from S.P.S. and got a job. Douglas was still an engineering student and almost failed because of an emergency appendectomy – in those days a serious operation, which many people did not survive. He was in the hospital for some time with complications, and his father visited him faithfully, often getting out of his own bed to do so.

As the new year, 1914, rolled along it became obvious that the Dean's health was failing. He was forced to miss more meetings, more dinners, more visits to other places. He did attend a dinner held in his honour in Ottawa, with more than 80 guests in attendance, but his wife and daughter went without him to the reception at Government House. His staff tried to spare him as much work and worry as possible, and he did much of his work from his bed. His family and friends all hoped that a summer spent at Go Home Bay would bring him back to health. It was not to be.

CHAPTER THIRTEEN

The Beauty of the Evening

JOHN AND EMILY GALBRAITH left for Go Home Bay early in July 1914. Beatrix and Jack were working in Toronto, but the youngest son, Douglas, accompanied them, still recuperating from his operation; his doctors felt a summer in the fresh air would be good for him. The family took its elderly setter, Paddy, and a young girl, named Grace, to help in the house. Emily made her annual purchase of leghorn chickens, to provide them with fresh eggs. Paddy remembered that he was not allowed to chase the chickens; after the first few days of rushing about, visiting old haunts and discovering new ones, even he was quieting down and was great company for the Dean.

Douglas varnished the dinghy and the canoe and started practising for the Regatta. He intended to try for first place again. On July 13, the Dean wrote to his daughter in Toronto that he was "somewhat improved ... certainly no worse." Friends dropped by to see him, and he depended on family to bring him the news from their daily visit to the community dock to pick up the mail. He learned about the good crop of blueberries and regretted that he could no longer climb the rock to see for himself – he was pretty well confined to the house and veranda. It was on the veranda, relaxing in an easy chair, that he spent most of his time, with a book in his hand and Paddy lying at his feet. Occasionally, when he felt well enough, the family went on a picnic with a few friends to one of the outlying islands. Douglas put a chair into the launch so that his father would have a comfortable place to sit when they reached their destination.

Then the weather changed, became extremely hot and muggy. Emily was worried because her husband was not well. She tried to protect him from visitors. The Spottons dropped over on Sunday, July 19, but he was unable to see them, and Douglas told friends who inquired at the dock about his father not to call. Emily wrote to her daughter on Tuesday, the 21st, that she was taking him to Toronto on Saturday for the doctor to see him. That afternoon Emily had tea at the Stuparts; then her nephew and niece rowed her home before going over to the dock to mail her letter and to pick up some things that had arrived by boat that day.

In the letter she told Beatrix that the hens were now laying well and that she had taken eggs over to Professor Ballantyne, who was also suffering from the heat. She expected the Saturday train to reach Toronto about 4.30 in the afternoon and requested Beatrix to have tea ready. She asked whether she should take another pair of blankets with her, as she intended to sleep with her daughter and wanted her husband to have all the blankets he needed. "You will have time to write me a card," she wrote.

That evening they had a late dinner on the veranda and enjoyed the beauty of the evening. Charlie Wright and his wife joined them to watch the setting sun, and the Dean remarked that no one could wish for a lovelier spot. A short time later, after he went to bed, he had a chill, but he soon felt better and insisted that he would be fine in the morning. However, about 4 a.m. Emily roused Douglas, and shortly afterward John Galbraith passed away peacefully, without waking from a quiet sleep.

In the morning Charlie Wright wired Hyman Irwin, managing editor of the *Canadian Engineer*, a former student and close personal friend. James Brebner, Registrar of the University, also wired his own office. The University community was stunned, for few realized how ill the Dean had been. Immediately the University flag was lowered to half-mast. Varsity was in mourning.

The family arrived in Toronto on the 3.45 train on Thursday, July 23, accompanying the body. They intended to have a private funeral service from their home at 57 Prince Arthur Avenue. John Galbraith had been a wonderful husband and father, and his family grieved, but he was not theirs alone. He belonged to the

University, and his students also claimed him as theirs and were not to be denied a last farewell to their "Beloved Dean." Plans were changed, and a private family service was held at his home at 1.30 p.m., followed by a public service at the Anglican Church of the Redeemer on the corner of Bloor Street and Avenue Road at 2.30 p.m., with Rev. C.J. James officiating.

Floral tributes arrived in such numbers that the house was a mass of flowers. Hundreds of telegrams piled up on the hall table. The Engineering Alumni Association took resposibility for their members from out-of-town, and the University looked after the horses and carriages for the family. It was the largest funeral seen in Toronto for years. Every branch of the Alumni Association and many class organizations sent representatives, who arrived from many parts of Canada and the United States. Engineers from Britain and other distant places wired to request that they be represented and sent magnificent floral tributes. Members of Government joined with hundreds of personal friends and undergraduates to pay tribute.

John Galbraith was buried in Mt. Pleasant Cemetery in Toronto, and later his sons arranged to have the rock he had enjoyed sitting on in front of his cottage at Go Home Bay taken to Midland by barge and from there by train to Toronto, where it now sits as the memorial stone on his burial site.

The Dean was dead, but his influence and his ideals continued on in the profession and the School to which he had dedicated his life.

A large portion of the publication *Applied Science* incorporated with *Transactions of the University of Toronto* (July 1914), was devoted to tributes to "Our Beloved Dean Galbraith." Besides being Principal and then Dean of S.P.S., he had also held many other positions of responsibility and trust. In his time he was Vice-President of the Association of Ontario Land Surveyors, of the Engineering Section of the B.A.A.S., of the American Association for the Advancement of Science, and of the Canadian Institute, Toronto. He was an associate member of Britain's Institute of Civil Engineers and a founder of the Canadian Society of Civil Engineers, serving as a Councillor for many years and President in 1909.

In September 1914 President Falconer stated, at an open meeting of the Engineering Society of Applied Science dedicated to Galbraith's memory, that he was a

thoroughly trustworthy man, thorough in training, honesty and patience. The engineering profession in Canada had lost a leader, the man considered to have done more for the profession in Canada than any other. The University had lost a man whose very name inspired confidence in the manufacturer and the commercial man alike, a man who had built up the "School" to stand amongst the foremost engineering colleges of the world. No student who graduated under the Dean ever had a problem finding work.

The students had lost a friend. The late Dean had appreciated undergraduates' capacity and position and in preparing the curriculum had always considered their needs first. The students trusted him as a person to whom they could always go with any difficulties or problems, and children loved him. The men with whom he came into contact or worked closely respected his opinion; in any disagreement, the decision usually went his way, because of his patience, tact, and strength of will.

The Dean of Engineering at McGill wrote: "He was not only a very able engineer, but a man of wide human sympathies and with a great power of inspiration." H.G. Tyrell, a Canadian and one of Galbraith's early students, wrote from his home in Evanston, Illinois: "Dr. Galbraith was one of the greatest men of his age, for he has been instrumental in producing the men who are now so strong a factor in the development of our Dominion." The Vice-President of the Foundation Company in New York said: "Dean Galbraith was the greatest practical engineering educator of his time, and, through his graduates, he has influenced all parts of the engineering world."

James Ross, a successful engineer, manager, and financier and a good judge of men, whom Galbraith had worked with as a young man, had said in 1883 that he was an exceptionally capable engineer and teacher and that any young man who was fortunate enough to graduate under his instruction needed no further collegiate training.

99

Emily's brother, R.F. Stupart, of the Meterological Service, stated that the Dean possessed more of the Christian virtues than any man he had ever known: "He was of a most kindly disposition, and was considerate, almost to a fault, of the feelings of all with whom he came in contact." Stupart could not recall him ever speaking unkindly of anyone, although he did show anger when he felt the cause justified it.

Another former student spoke for many when he wrote:

First as a pupil and afterwards as one of the many who had the good fortune to possess his friendship, I grew to respect more and more and admire those rare qualities of heart and mind which so endeared him to all who knew him.

His personality was extremely attractive. He appealed to all sorts and conditions of people, to young and old, to the plain workman as well as to the educated college man.

He had all the qualities of a truly great leader. He had wonderful tact and intuition and was very, very kindly. His modesty and genial, good nature, keen sense of humour, and charity for human weaknesses, gained him friends everywhere, and yet when necessary, he could be very strong, but he ruled through love and not through force.

He possessed the faculty to a remarkable degree of imparting knowledge to others, and of stimulating a desire for thoroughness. I have met none who were his equal in this respect. There was something in him which unconsciously brought out the best in his pupils. I do not remember that he ever lectured his class on conduct or ethics; but his influence somehow stimulated the best that was in us. He was not only a great teacher of Applied Science – he was an upbuilder of character – he made Men as well as Engineers.

John A. Brashear wrote from Pittsburgh:

The last time I met the dear fellow was when he visited "his boys" in my native city of Pittsburgh, for in this great centre of engineering interests many of his graduate students have made an honourable name for themselves, and no man was more gloried and honoured than was Dr. Galbraith by "his boys" in Pittsburgh.

Canada has given us many worthy names to be written high in the hall of fame, but none greater than this good man, who has given his life for the advancement of science – for the betterment of human interests, for the higher ideals of citizenship, and for that purer and nobler manhood that gives us new faith in our kind, and prompts us all to say: "A good man has gone from among us."

The first meeting of the Engineering Society after the Dean's death was dedicated to his memory. Person after person rose to speak of the Dean's work and interject personal memories of him. Charlie Wright invited Kennard Thompson, a consulting engineer in New York and an S.P.S. graduate of 1886, to pay tribute to his former teacher. Dr. Thompson said that there was no man living whom he respected, admired, and loved as much as he did Dean Galbraith. Thompson had good cause to feel gratitude. He had a hearing impairment and during his school days struggled to get through classes. His professor knew of his difficulty and, without letting anyone else become aware of it, made sure that Thompson always sat in the front row. Thompson spoke of his teacher's life from childhood on, interspersed with anecdotes from his own student days:

The Dean never said in actual words that he expected everyone to be honest, truthful and faithful to his employers, employees, family and friends, yet everyone felt that he fully expected such behaviour.

He used stories to put his point across and the listener was not aware at the time of the moral values he was learning. In speaking to a child he quoted verses from Pinafore to illustrate how industry was rewarded.

The Engineering Society, Canada's oldest, had always been dear to the heart of the Dean, and he never missed the annual banquet. They were always well attended, for graduates looked forward to listening to Galbraith speak. At one banquet, when the students were having a serious disagreement with the faculty and were exceptionally unruly, Galbraith outlined the problem and then told a story about an Irishman who was riding a mule. The mule tried every trick he could think of to shake his rider off, with no success, until he managed to catch one of his hind feet in the stirrup. Pat looked down and said, "Begorra, if you are going to get up, I think that I had better get off; but," Galbraith continued, "I can assure the students that the faculty is not going to get off." As usual, he had struck the right note, and with laughter and applause the disruption ended.

In 1909, after the joint banquet of the Society and the C.S.C.E. a group had been talking about how successful the event was. One graduate from another university asked why his college could not do one as well. "The answer is simple," replied a fellow graduate. "You have no Galbraith."

Dr. Thompson was not the only speaker at the meeting, and each person who spoke added his tribute to a friend and teacher. At the end of the evening, the seed was planted for a fitting memorial. It took years for it to grow.

W.H. Ellis was appointed as Dean to follow Galbraith. He had been part of the original teaching staff at S.P.S., and the two men had been close friends. Ellis was well acquainted with the ideals and aspirations of Dean Galbraith, and for much of the last year of John's life had been unobtrusively doing a lot of the work. He had been one of the few people aware of his friend's failing health. He was, perhaps, not as strong and dominant a character but was well qualified for the position, respected and loved by students and colleagues alike. The foundation had been well laid, and Dean Ellis was ready to carry it on.

In 1927 the Engineering Alumni Association of the University of Toronto struck a Galbraith Memorial Committee to provide a fitting tribute. After much discussion, the Committee decided to have a bronze portrait bust commissioned, to be dedicated on the fiftieth anniversary of the beginning of S.P.S. On February 18, 1927, letters went out to all alumni, requesting two dollars from all pre–1914 graduates, who knew the Dean personally, and one dollar from those who had graduated after 1914. Contributions flowed in. Many sent donations of $10.00 to $25.00, with covering letters telling of their feelings for their teacher and offering more money if needed.

From Gravenhurst, Ontario, a graduate of 1910 wrote: "It would be difficult to overestimate what 'The School' owes to its old friend

'Johnnie', and I am sure your appeal to its graduates, especially those who were privileged to study under him, should meet with a ready response. Thanking you for the privilege of subscribing." From St. Marys, Ontario: "As the years pass by, one appreciates more and more what he did for those of us who were fortunate enough to receive instruction in the old S.P.S." Another wrote: "I was one of those fortunate enough to be rather intimately associated with Dr. Galbraith and I can say, in all sincerity and humbleness, that the memory of him has helped over many a tight place." A graduate of 1908 from Erie, Pennsylvania, summed up the feelings of many in his letter enclosing his subscription: "Truly he was a great power among the students, and I can think of nothing more fitting in connection with the Fiftieth Anniversary of the School than that a suitable memorial be dedicated to his memory." More than 800 people subscribed.

Canadian sculptor Emmanuel Hahn was commissioned to execute a sculpture of the head and shoulders. It was made of bronze, and all the modelling and casting were done in Toronto. The memorial was mounted on a simple pedestal of dark marble, with only Galbraith's name and the dates of his birth and death inscribed. The finished bust was placed against the wall opposite the door of the Mining Building under his portrait.

The unveiling, in the autumn of 1927, was an impressive ceremony, held in conjunction with the fiftieth anniversary of S.P.S. and the centenary of the University of Toronto. The lobby of the Mining Building was full to overflowing when J.M.R. Fairbairn, Chief Engineer of the Canadian Pacific Railway and President of the Engineering Alumni Association, unveiled the bust. President Canon Cody accepted on behalf of the University and spoke highly of the Dean's achievements. His true memorial, however, was to be found in the love and admiration of thousands of his former students.

Professor Vander Smissen, a lifelong friend, who also summered at Go Home Bay and who had been a member of the Arts Faculty while Galbraith was at the School, was unable to attend the ceremony and sent a beautiful wreath, which sat at the base of the pedestal for the unveiling. Beatrix Galbraith, with her husband and two daughters, and Jack and his wife were honoured guests.

Emily had died in 1917, and Douglas in 1920, of a chronic problem complicated by wounds suffered during the Great War.

As the years went on, more and more students entered the Faculty of Applied Science and Engineering, and new buildings sprouted on the Campus. Finally the Little Red School House had outlived its usefulness and was torn down. The lintels, the name, and some of the bricks were saved and set into the wall at the entrance and in the quadrangle of the new Engineering building on St. George Street. The new home was named for John Galbraith, and his bust was moved to a place of honour in the foyer. Here the founder of S.P.S. still presides in spirit over new generations of prospective engineers.

Address by Dean Galbraith, Retiring President of the Canadian Society of Civil Engineers, delivered at the Annual Meeting of the Society in Toronto, January, 27, 1909.

Gentlemen, – Custom in this Society demands of the retiring president, whether wisely or otherwise, it is not for me to say, an address at the close of his term of office. Fortunately for him no by-law exists governing either the form or matter of his essay. He is not required to confine himself to the third person and has all the freedom implied in the declaration, printed in every volume of the "Transactions," that the "Society will not hold itself responsible for any statements or opinions which may be advanced in the following pages." Answerable thus to no one and confined only by my natural limitations, I jotted down from time to time, by way of gathering material, ideas as they occurred to me. When a sufficient number had accumulated to enable me to form a judgement of their suitability for the purpose in view, I was dismayed to find that my stock was shopworn and that it would not be an easy task to work it into presentable shape. However, it was then too late to throw it away. After a period of severe reflection I convinced myself that it might be of some value to the younger members of the profession and that even the seniors might be interested in the viewpoint of an engineering teacher, differing as it does in many respects from their own. I decided, therefore, to form my material into a paper under the somewhat hackneyed title of "The Engineer and His Work."

In tracing backwards the history of the engineer to classical times, two words stand out with marked prominence – unxav'n and ingenium. The root idea of the former is contrivance, resource, ways and means; of the latter, nature, intelligence, ingenuity. The phrase "mechanical genius" describes the highest attribute of the engineer, the control of mind over matter, the power of bending the forces of nature to the use and convenience of man. The antiquity of the words and the continued application of their derivatives down to the present day to the same set of ideas are evidence that the art and craft of the engineer are not of yesterday nor the outcome of modern conditions. The remains of the great structures of ancient civilization – temples and amphitheatres, baths, aqueducts and sewers, walled cities and military roads, are witnesses to the genius of engineers whose names have been long forgotten, of men skilled in surveying, levelling, drawing, hydraulics, excavation and construction. The entrenched camp, the tunnelled approach, the battering-ram catapult and moving tower were the devices of the engineer. He had a great part then as now in the arts of peace and war.

An inscription on a marble altar discovered in 1866 near Lambaese, Algeria, of date A.D.152, contains a petition from Varius Clemens, governor of Mauritania, to Valerius Etruscus, governor of Numidia. It reads as follows:

Varius Clemens greets Valerius Etruscus and begs him in his own name and in the name of the township of Saldae to dispatch at once the hydraulic engineer of the Third Legion Nonius Datus with orders that he finish the work which he seems to have forgotten.

The petition was favorably received by the governor and by the engineer Nonius Datus, who when he had fulfilled his mission wrote to the magistrates of Saldae the following report;

After leaving my quarters I met with brigands on my way, who robbed me even of my clothes and wounded me severely. I succeeded after the encounter in reaching Saldae where I was met by the governor, who after allowing me some rest took me to the tunnel. There I found everybody sad and despondent; they had given up all hopes that the two opposite sections of the tunnel would meet, because each section had already been excavated beyond the middle of the mountain and the junction had not yet been effected. As always happens in these cases, the fault was attributed to the engineer, as though he had not taken all precautions to ensure the success of the work. What could I have done better? I began by surveying and taking levels of the mountain: I marked most carefully the axis of the tunnel across the ridge; I drew plans and sections of the whole work, which plans I handed over to Petronius Celer, then governor of Mauritania; and to take extra precaution I summoned the contractor and his workmen and began the excavation in their presence with the help of two gangs of experienced veterans, namely a detachment of marine infantry and a detachment of Alpine troops. What more could I have done? Well during the four years I was absent at Lambaese expecting every day to hear the good tidings of the arrival of the waters at Saldae, the contractor and the assistant had committed blunder upon blunder; in each section of the tunnel they had diverged from the straight line, each towards his right; had I waited a little longer before coming, Saldae would have possessed two tunnels instead of one.

Nonius Datus, having discovered the mistake, caused the two diverging arms to be united by a transverse tunnel; the waters of the Ain-seur could finally cross the mountain and their arrival at Saldae was celebrated with extraordinary rejoicings in the presence of the governor, Varius Clemens, and of the engineer. (Lanciani-Ancient Rome in the Light of Modern Discoveries.) We can, I am sure, sympathize with our confrere the engineer of the Third Legion in his difficulties, and rejoice with him in his triumph.

The Romans as a rule constructed their aqueducts with grades approaching those of our modern railways. They tunnelled mountains and bridged valleys, not, it must be remembered, that they were ignorant of the fact that water could be carried across valleys in inverted siphons, but because they were unacquainted with the use of cast iron. There is at least one instance of a masonry or perhaps a concrete pipe constructed by the Romans which was able to withstand pressures as high as ten atmospheres.

The first advance in engineering after the time of the Romans was due to the invention of gunpowder in the beginning of the fourteenth century, or perhaps it may be more correct to say, to its introduction into Europe about that time. By it the methods of excavation and of attack and defence were revolutionized.

The next great step was the introduction of iron as a structural material, which was rendered possible by the use of coke as a blast furnace fuel in the early part of the eighteenth century. Following the manufacture of coke iron came Watt's epoch-making improvements in the steam engine in the latter part of the same century – the separate condenser, expansive action, the double acting cylinder, the steam jacket, the parallel motion, the throttle valve, the governor, the water guage, the indicator, and many others. Watt also conceived and patented in 1782 the idea of the compound engine, which he thus described: "A new compound engine or method of connecting together the cylinders and condensers of two or more distinct engines so as to make the steam which has been employed to press on the piston of the first act expansively on the piston of the second, etc." Watt, in fact, gave the world the steam engine which exists today, the improvements made since his time being as nothing compared with his. The achievements and personality of James Watt cannot be better described than in the words of Sir Walter Scott after meeting him in 1818:

There were assembled about half a score of our Northern Lights . . . Amidst this company stood Mr. Watt, the man whose genius discovered the means of multiplying our national resources to a degree perhaps even beyond his own stupendous powers of calculation and combination; bringing the treasures of the abyss to the summit of the earth – giving the feeble arm of man the momentum of an Afrite – commanding manufactures to arise as the rod of the prophet produced water in the desert – affording the means of dispensing with that time and tide which wait for no man and of sailing without that wind which defied the commands and threats of Xerxes himself.

This potent commander of the elements, this abridger of time and space – this magician whose cloudy machinery has produced a change on the world, the effects of which, extraordinary as they are, are perhaps only now beginning to be felt, was not only the most profound man of science, the most successful combiner of powers and calculator of numbers as adapted to practical purposes – was not only one of the most generally well-informed, but one of the best and kindest of human beings.

There he stood, surrounded by the little band I have mentioned of northern literati, men not less tenacious generally speaking of their own fame and their own opinions than the national regiments are supposed to be jealous of the high character they have won upon service. Methinks I yet see and hear what I shall never see or hear again. In his eighty-second year the alert, kind, benevolent old man had his attention alive to every one's question, his information at every one's command. His talents and fancy overflowed on every subject. One gentleman was a deep philologist – he talked with him on the origin of the alphabet as if he had been coeval with Cadmus – another a celebrated critic – you would have said the old man had studied political economy and belles-lettres all his life – of science it is unnecessary to speak, it was his own distinguished walk. And yet, Captain Clutterbuck, when he spoke with your countryman, Jedediah Cleishbotham, you would have sworn he had been coeval with Claver'se and Burley with the persecutors and persecuted and could number every shot the dragoons had fired at the fugitive Covenanters. In fact we discovered that no novel of the least celebrity escaped his perusal, and that the gifted man of science was as much addicted to the productions of your native country, in other words as shameless and obstinate a peruser of novels as if he had been a very miller's apprentice of eighteen.

One scarcely knows which to wonder at most, the genius of the engineer or the vision of the poet.

Sir Humphrey Davy said of Watt: "He was equally distinguished as a natural philosopher and a chemist and his inventions demonstrate his profound knowledge of these sciences." – (Muirhead's Life of James Watt.)

Watt was not only the greatest of mechanical engineers – he was an expert surveyor and civil engineer as well. He spent several years of his life in making surveys and reports on harbors, docks, canals, water works, bridges, etc. He invented a quadrant, a surveyor's micrometer, clock and other instruments of precision. As an illustration of the rate of pay of civil engineers in 1770, Watt's charge for the survey of the Strathmore Canal may be of interest. The field work covered 43 days for which he charged 80 pounds including travelling and living expenses; for the preparation of the report he was paid the further sum of 30 pounds.

The manufacture of iron on the large scale has been accompanied within the last thirty years by an enormous expansion in the manufacture of Portland cement and the consequent return to the use of concrete as a structural material. Within the same period the development of the dynamo has marked another advance comparable in importance only with that of the steam engine. It is not to be supposed, however, that these modern features have entirely absorbed the energies of the engineering and industrial world. Few of the ancient arts and manufactures have lost their importance. They have undergone development and transformation under the light of modern science and the stimulus of modern conditions. Through all these changes man, their author, seems to survive almost unchanged. The human race, civilized or savage, is, man for man, very much the same as it was three thousand years ago. Nonius Datus had the full qualifications for admission into the Canadian Society of Civil Engineers. No one would recognize any essential difference between him and other members, except perhaps that he was better educated, being able to talk Latin.

It will be unnecessary to recite to an audience of engineers in any minute detail the various fields of activity now open to the profession. It may be useful, however, to attempt a classification of the functions of the engineer irrespective of the special branch in which he may be engaged. They may be roughly analyzed as follows:

1. Design – the preparation of the drawings, specifications and estimates of cost for works not yet in existence – the study of the problem, the devising of ways and means – in short, the consideration of all questions affecting the construction and efficiency of the contemplated work.

2. Survey and inspection – making the examination of existing works or ground for the purpose of determining necessary extensions and changes – laying out new work – measuring work done – inspection of materials and workmanship, and generally, the superintendence of construction.

3. Superintendence of the operation and maintenance of works in running condition.

4. Determining and estimating costs of various kinds.

5. Reporting upon various physical and financial features of existing or proposed works.

To successfully perform these functions the engineer must have knowledge, training, experience, judgement, resourcefulness, business capacity and ability to deal with men, in fact the qualifications which are necessary for success in any line of life. It goes without saying that he should be an educated man in the best sense of the term. It has sometimes been said that the engineer should be forty percent. engineer and sixty per cent. man; one might better say that he should be one hundred per cent. engineer and one hundred per cent. man not being, it is to be hoped, mutually exclusive. It is necessary that he should have a thorough grasp of the objects and methods of the promoters and proprietors of the works on which he is engaged and be quick to discern where expense may be saved, keeping the necessary efficiency in view. It is not requisite that he be an expert mathematician, chemist, physicist, geologist, biologist, metallurgist, mechanic, accountant, lawyer or political economist, but it is desirable that he be an expert engineer. For this purpose he should have a sound acquaintance with the principles and possibilities of various branches of specialized knowledge in so far as they bear upon his own work. In other words, he should have a clear perception of how and how much these branches may aid him in his own problems and be able to determine at any time to whom he should go when his own knowledge is insufficient. He must know the limitations of his own profession and therefore should know something of the fields which surround his own. Often it happens that some particular fence has almost disappeared and it becomes difficult to determine where the engineer ends and the neighboring proprietor begins. Indeed, it may be said that the fences are continually changing so that the engineer never can hope to be in the position of not requiring to study non-engineering things. The training to be given in the engineering schools should deal more with subjects which are not engineering than with those which are, the reason being that the time for such training is short whereas that to be devoted to engineering is long. Above all, the curriculum should be educative, the student should be trained in clear thinking and in clear expression. When he graduates he should have acquired a sufficient knowledge of his geography to have some idea of where he is in the world in general and in the engineering world in particular. It is now recognized that the study of the applied sciences has all the educational advantages usually attributed to that of the pure sciences. They involve the same principles, exercise the same faculties and produce the same educational results as the pure sciences. The fact that their objects are wholly economic does not detract from their educational value but provides an additional stimulus to scientific effort. The term "applied science," at one time suitable, is now rather misleading in connection with the science taught in the engineering schools. It suggests the idea that the business of the teachers in these schools is to train their students in the application to practical purposes of pure science. This is far from being the truth. The necessities of the practical world have developed great bodies of science with which the investigators in pure science are more or less unacquainted and are unable to take part in, either in the way of investigation or teaching, on account of the natural limitations of time, opportunity and taste. The term "practical" better

111

described the engineering and technical sciences and the term "applied" should be discontinued in this connection. The practical sciences are taught in the engineering schools and are applied by the engineer in his work. The teachers of practical science should keep in touch with the requirements of engineers and manufacturers and not develop merely into laboratory investigators following their own lines of thought, indifferent to where these may lead. This is right and proper in the region of pure science, but those engaged in practical science must deny themselves the pleasures of unrestricted freedom. They cannot afford to soar too long in the clouds but must return again and again to earth. They must never forget that their only reason for being is the assistance they give as educators or investigators to the actual workers in the industrial fields. It is essential for the success of their work that they should be officially independent of the teachers in pure science in the university organization. They should have experience in engineering work, not for the purpose of teaching it, for there is little engineering which can be profitably taught in a school, but in order that they may be able to properly direct their true work, the teaching and investigation of practical science.

The engineer is not simply an applier of the sciences. He comes into contact with men as well as with things. He should understand the principles underlying commerce and finance, company organization, cost keeping and accounts. A financial statement ought not to be a mystery to him nor a railway report past understanding. He should have, at least, as clear a conception of the meaning of a contract as the lawyer who drafted it. He should be able to write a report in clear and expressive English. The engineering schools are beginning to understand that these subjects are not altogether above and beyond them, nor yet beneath them. It is true that an expert businessman cannot be trained in a school; no more can an expert engineer. Business science, however, can be taught just as successfully as chemistry or physics. Businessmen are said to have a prejudice against academic training in business. Engineers once had a similar prejudice against engineering schools. With a better understanding of their field on the part of the schools will come a better appreciation on the part of the businessman. The schools should devote their energies to the teaching of principles. The teaching of practical methods should be chiefly for the purpose of making the connection between theory and practice, thus clarifying and impressing the principles on the student's mind.

One of the most difficult subjects in the curriculum is English. It should not be taught as are French and German for the purpose of giving the student access to its literature, engineering or otherwise. Students can, as a rule get the information they want from English books without the aid of a professor of English. The object in teaching English in the engineering school should not be to give the student a grasp of the principles underlying the formation of words and sentences. It should be assumed that his high school training in grammar is sufficient for this purpose. The instruction most necessary under present conditions is training in the use of the language. However, there may be a better way. There does not seem to be any good reason why the course of instruction in English in this country should not be turned end for end. Why should not the secondary school teach the boy to use his mother tongue and the university teach grammar?

One of the dangers to be avoided in the academic course of the engineer is over-specialization. It should be remembered that the graduate does not always find work in the branch to which he has devoted his four years of academic life. If his course, therefore, has not included a reasonable number of subjects more or less common to all branches of engineering he will have good cause of complaint against the educational authorities. A properly educated graduate ought to be able by his own reading to adapt himself to any situation wherein he may be placed. A broad education is the best preparation for specialization in after life.

The academic requirements for young men entering the profession would be better determined by the discussions of practising engineers than of any other body of men, and yet they seem to have little or nothing to say on the subject. There seems to be something in the work of the engineer which suppresses talk, even useful talk. This is very well in a way but may be carried too far. Engineers ought not to hide their light under a bushel and expect the world to reward them for their silent work's sake. The world is too busy a man to study engineering and would perhaps take more interest in engineers if they were to take the trouble to explain things. However, this disability is probably on the decrease owing to the influence of the engineering schools; and engineers are not as silent as they once were. They show signs of awakening and will not long be content to act simply as advisers or scientific hired men, indifferent to the big world as long as they get their pay. The engineer of the future will force his ideas of engineering education on the public and force them more effectively than his predecessors of the past and present.

The engineer should have a thorough knowledge of the materials with which he has to deal. The laboratory investigations of the chemist, the physicist and the biologist have added greatly to the store of knowledge at his disposal. Laboratory results, however, often require modification in as much as the artificial conditions surrounding them may differ essentially from the conditions of practical work. Thus it is not sufficient to accept materials of construction simply because they have passed the specified short time tests. The engineer should know in addition as much as possible of the history of his materials, their sources, methods of manufacture, modes of growth, etc.; without this knowledge the rapid examinations in the laboratory and testing room may altogether fail in their purpose of excluding unsuitable materials. Similarly in construction, it is not sufficient to examine the completed work and see that it complies with certain specified final conditions. It is necessary to watch the whole process of manufacture and construction from the beginning to the end. In other words, no short time tests or inspections will relieve the engineer from the necessity of knowing the whole history of his materials and construction. It is this fact which has forced on the profession what one may call standardized materials and methods of construction developed from experience. New materials and new processes are wisely looked upon with distrust and can achieve success only after a long period of trial. The life of a structure or machine is not only shortened by imperfections of material and workmanship and the corroding action of the elements, but by being subjected to heavier service than was anticipated in the original design. The engineer must therefore combine the functions of the prophet and the actuary and decide to what present expense it is worth while going in view of future contingencies.

There is more or less doubt in the minds of engineers as to the degree to which details of workmanship, manufacture, modes of construction, materials, etc., should be covered in their specifications. The only answer is "that depends." Where in these respects standardization has taken place and the engineer knows that the results are good, the task of specifying is comparitively simple. Much may be left to the contractor and manufacturer. Where, on the contrary, customary methods and materials are not appropriate to the work, the specifications of the engineer must be given in greater detail. Thus between the extremes of simply specifying the results desired, leaving methods and materials to those who do the work, and specifying how everything is to be done and the actual materials to be used there is wide latitude, and the medium to be adopted in every case depends largely on general conditions of available manufaturing and contracting skill and capacity. Whatever may be the degree of detail to which he may carry his specifications the engineer cannot be relieved from the obligation of being well acquainted with the current practice of manufacturing and contracting firms, and with the materials with which he has to deal whether they be materials of construction or obstruction. The young graduate can have no better position in which to gain experience than that of contractor's engineer.

It would be well for specifications to cover not only the work to be performed by the contractor but also the data and assumptions underlying the engineer's project. While not absolutely necessary for the prosecution of the work, such information would be useful to the profession and for future reference, not to speak of its effect upon the engineer himself in increasing his sense of responsibility. The different classes of drawings referred to in the contract should be carefully defined in the specifications, otherwise ambiguities and uncertainties in interpretation will arise. Drawings may be looked upon as a species of shorthand invented to save words, time and expense, and the engineer should be an expert in reading drawings, and in writing them in such a way as to convey his exact meaning. Correct drawings and correct English both imply a competent knowledge of the subject of which they are the expression.

The engineer should know the cost of the work done under his supervision, not merely the cost to the proprietor, for that goes without saying, but also as far as possible the cost to the contractor. Not only should he keep in touch with the labor market, but he should take and interest in the physical and social welfare of the men under his charge. They should look upon him as a friend and not as an impersonal being concerned only in the results of their work. As between the contractor and the proprietor he must occupy the position of an impartial judge and not that of an advocate. The more thoroughly he knows his work the better able will he be to do his duty in this respect, and to retain the confidence of both parties. His knowledge of law and business should be sufficient to enable him to act harmoniously with those in charge of the legal and commercial intersects connected with his work. In fine he must be a many-sided man, thoroughly acquainted with his own side of the work and able to cooperate with all sorts and conditions of men.

Engineers are naturally divided into classes according to the special nature of their work. For the purpose of mutual improvement in their specialties, these classes form societies, of which the main features are the reading of papers, the interchange of ideas and the extension of persona acquaintance. While these societies do a vast amount of good within their own spheres they are not capable of dealing with the question of the improvement of the engineering profession as a whole. The Canadian Society of Civil Engineers was formed in 1887 with this object. The charter reads: "The Canadian Society of Civil Engineers having for its objects and proposes to facilitate the acquirement and interchange of professional knowledge among its members and more particularly to promote the acquisition of that species of knowledge which has special reference to the profession of civil engineering, and further to encourage investigation in connection with all branches and departments of knowledge connected with the profession," etc.

The second by-law reads; "The term Civil Engineer as used in this Society shall mean all who are or have been, engaged in the designing or constructing of railways, canals, harbors, lighthouses, bridges, roads, river improvements or other hydraulic works, sanitary, electrical, mining, mechanical or military works or in the study and practice of navigation by water or air, or in the directing of the great sources of power in nature for the use and convenience of man."

It must be confessed after an existence of twenty-one years that the Canadian Society has not succeeded in gaining recognition by the various classes of engineers in the country as the representative and authoritative engineering society. Even in England the term "civil engineering" has not gained full recognition as embracing all branches of the profession.

The "New English Dictionary" edited by Sir James Murray and recognized as one of the greatest authorities on the language, gives among others the following definitions of the word engineer:

2b. One who designs and constructs military works for attack or defence.
3. One whose profession is the designing and constructing of works of public utility such as bridges, roads, canals, railways, harbors, drainage works, gas and waterworks, etc. From 18th century also civil engineer, not in Johnson 1775 or

116

Todd 1818. The former has only the military sense to which the latter adds 'a maker of engines,' citing Bullokar.

In the early quotations the persons referred to were probably by profession military engineers though the works mentioned were of a 'civil' character. Since 2b. has ceased to be a prominent sense of engineer the term 'civil engineer' has lost its original antithetic force but it continues to be the ordinary designation of the profession to which it was first applied, distinguishing it from that of mechanical engineer. Other phraseological combinations, as electric, gas mining, railway, telegraph engineers are used to designate those who devote themselves to special departments of engineering.

1792 Smeaton, Reports(1797) 1 Pref.7. The first meeting of this new institution, the Society of Civil Engineers, was held on the 15th of April, 1793.

1793 Edystone L. Introd.8 "my profession of a civil engineer."

As Smeaton died in 1792, the dates 1797 and 1793 are probably the dates of publication of the reports. According to Sir Alexander Binnie, the first society of civil engineers in England was formed in London about the year 1760 by engineers who were in attendance at the Session of Parliament.

It seems, therefore, that the term "civil engineer" in England dates from about 1760 and that in the opinion of the editor of the New English Dictionary, who may be assumed to represent the public, it applies at present to engineers having to do with works of public utility such as those mentioned, but it is to be distinguished from the term mechanical engineer.

The same tendency to restriction of the term "civil engineer" exists in Canada and the United States not only among the public but in the profession as well. In all the great engineering schools this tendency is reflected.

The question now arises, is it worth while to expend further energy in resisting what appears to be a natural tendency? The only reason for the introduction of the term "civil" was that the word "engineer" had previously been monopolized by those engaged in military works; now that this distinction has lost its importance, would it not be better to drop the term "civil" as applied to the whole profession and confine it to the special applications justified by modern custom?

The profession as a whole should be represented in Canada by a single authoritative body somewhat after the pattern of the Medical Council or the Benchers of the Law Society in Ontario, to which should be entrusted the subjects of engineering education, qualifications for professional standing, professional ethics, etc., in short all questions of general professional interest. It is only by the hearty co-operation of the various classes of engineers that such a movement could succeed. The Canadian Society of Engineers with its Council would thus exercise functions which are necessary for the strengthening of the profession in its relations with the public, and which lie outside the province of the special engineering societies.

As a rule the engineer does not come immediately into contact with the public. At the same time there are questions of public interest in which he, in common with the chemist, the metallurgist, the biologist, the medical practitioner, the forester and others, is regarded as an authority. The public expects the engineer to aid by his advice in the improvement of transportation, the prevention of railway accidents, the abatement of smoke, the preservation and improvement of public health, transmission of power, the irrigation of arid lands, the economical management and conservation of forests and mines, the improvement of agricultural soils, the conservation of river flow, etc., etc. Such questions are matters of municipal and governmental policy and cannot be properly controlled by money-making corporations or individuals. Before a move can be made in these matters a strong body of enlightened public opinion must be formed, and who should be better qualified for the task of stimulating and guiding this public opinion than the engineer? If he is too busy or too backward to undertake this duty of his own accord, what about the editor of the engineering newspaper? The latter is never hampered by modesty and should write not only for his subscribers but for the public as well. He need not fear that his work will be lost; the lay press will print his good articles and give him due credit for them.

Mr. Carnegie is reported to have made the statement that at the present rate of consumption, the supply of iron ore (presumably the more important and richer ores) of the United States would be exhausted in forty years and the supply in England within seven years. He based this opinion on the best expert evidence he could obtain. If this statement be correct, what a prospect does it not open for the vast iron resources of Canada, and yet at the same time what a warning does it not convey to the government which controls these resources! In the United States the total production of pig iron up to the present is 350,000,000 tons of which over one-half has been made within the last ten years. The production of the world in 1907 was 61,000,000 tons, of which the United States are to be credited with 26,000,000, Germany with 13,000,000, Great Britain with 10,000.000 and other countries with 11,000,000. Canada produced 600,000 tons less than one per cent. of the total. In the United States the acid Bessemer process seems to have reached its maximum output and in the future will rapidly diminish in importance owing to the increasing scarcity of the requisite ores and its inability to use scrap. It is being rapidly superceded by the basic open hearth process, which can utilize ores containing a larger percentage of phosphorus and also all kinds of scrap.

The future of electric processes in iron and steel production in Canada will depend more upon the cost of hydro-electric power than on any other factor. Closely connected with the conservation of the iron and timber resources of America is the great Portland cement industry, which has sprung into importance with the last twenty years. The Canadian production in 1907 amounted to 2,400,000 barrels, the United States production to 49,000,000 barrels. Concrete and ferro concrete will replace steel and wood in construction in ever increasing quantities. As in the case of the electrometallurgy of iron, the cost of hydro-electric power is a large item in the manufacture of cement.

The conservation and regulation of river-flow for water power alone, to say nothing of transportation and irrigation, is a necessity for the future industries of the country. The regularity and volume of river-flow in its turn is dependent upon the preservation of forest growth, especially in the mountainous and upland regions. Forest conservation in fact is one of the fundamental conditions of future prosperity. And so one might go on, and enumerate one after the other, various sources of wealth and well-being now extravagantly exploited which demand for their wise development the knowledge and skill of the engineer. It is to be hoped that the conferences initiated by President Roosevelt to consider the conservation of natural resources will bear fruit in pointing the way to practical solutions of these national problems. Canada has already made a good beginning both in collecting information regarding our resources and in passing legislation.

One of the most striking illustrations of modern economic tendencies is the increase which has taken place in the voltage of power transmission lines. Within the last twenty-five years the practicable voltage has been increased from 1,000 to 110,000 volts, thus immensely extending the possible area of distribution from the hydro-electric power plant.

In the machine shop, complex machine tools, largely the inventions of the mechanic, high speed tool steels, electric motor drives and high class organization have immensely increased the output and decreased unit costs. The steam turbine, the improved hydraulic turbine, electric lighting, electric traction, the gas engine, the great ocean and lake freighters, the monster liners and that concentrated essence of power, the modern battleship, have all come within the present generation and we cannot predict what changes in the application of power and machinery will take place before it passes away. It would not be surprising if the automobile were to displace electric transportation in cities and be replaced for purposes of pleasure by the aeroplane and the dirigible balloon. In the future, electric transportation may be confined to underground tunnels in the cities and largely replace steam power on railway lines through the country. Evidently the end of the work of the engineer is not yet at hand. The inventions of the present day, under the stimulus of science and the ever-increasing complexity of life, crowd so closely upon us that it is impossible to form a just estimate of their relative values. That must be left to the judgement of posterity looking backward through the long perpective of the years.

One of the first duties of a country is to work up within its own limits its raw materials into the forms in which they are to be finally used by individual consumers. Only in so far as this end is successfully accomplished will the manufacturing population of a country be increased and the cost of transportation of its products to a foreign country, in comparison with their value, be diminished. One effect of over-production or decreased profits is to stimulate invention for the purpose of reducing the cost of production and transportation. As a rule the first effect is to throw labor out of employment, but this is no argument against invention. Wages will fall in any case owing to the failing market for the product, and can be maintained only by the discovery of new markets. The decrease of cost due to labor-saving inventions leads to the extension of the markets without which production must be checked and labor seek new fields, or be reduced to a lower standard of living. Thus a country depends for material prosperity as much upon the brains of its scientific men, inventors and engineers as upon its natural resources. Money spent upon unproductive enterprises means waste of labour and the stoppage before long of the wheels of industry. Capital knows no country; it ever flows to the land of promise; let it be our endeavor to make Canada no mere land of promise but a land of fulfilment as well. Fortunate in possessing vast agricultural resources without which no nation can be self-sustaining , Canada can afford to take time in developing its mines. The mines are our treasure houses, which once emptied, can never again be filled – while the scattered gold, silver, copper and iron that remain in the country may to some extent be recovered after having fulfilled their first uses, the coal, oil, and gas once used are gone forever.

The preservation of our fisheries and forest demands our first attention. Their cultivation must begin and their mining must cease, if we are not to lose them altogether. Nor need the engineer fear that under such a policy his opportunities would be deferred or his field narrowed. The conservation of our resources will introduce many new problems, will stimulate research and invention, cheapen production, open up new markets and enable the country to sustain a much larger and more permanent population than we have any right to expect from a continuance of our present ill regulated and short-sighted practice of extravagant consumption and waste.

In conclusion I have to thank the members of the Society for the honor they conferred upon me a year ago in electing me to the highest office within their gift, an honor altogether undeserved on the score of previous service. I have also to thank my colleagues of the outgoing council for the kindly assistance which I have in many ways received from them in the performance of my special duties. I am sure that they join me in wishing the new council an increased measure of success in promoting the interests of the Society.

Applied Science, New Series, Vol. 11, Number 4, February, 1909.
University of Toronto Archives, Toronto, Ontario

NOTE ON SOURCES

The material for John Galbraith's home life, his professional life, his summer and recreational activities came from the articles, newspaper clippings, correspondence and his personal diaries saved through the years by his daughter and son, and from personal reminiscences of his daughter. The originals or copies of all the papers are in the John Galbraith file (B78-0018/001), University of Toronto Archives (hereafter UTA), University of Toronto, Ontario.

The sources for engineering education in Toronto throughout the book are as follows:

- James Loudon Papers (872-0031), UTA
- Reports on Education in Ontario in the late 19th and 20th centuries, Ontario Archives, Toronto
- *Torontonensis*, 1889, 1901, 1911
- C.R. Young, *Early Engineering Education at Toronto 1851–1919* (Toronto: University of Toronto Press 1958)

Sources regarding the Madawaska Club and Go Home Bay came from the following books published privately by members of the Madawaska Club, copies of which are stored in the UTA:

- W.J. Loudon, *A Short History of the Founding of the Madawaska Club and Its Early Settlement at Go Home Bay 1898–1903*
- *The Madawaska Club, Go Home Bay, 1897–1923* (Toronto 1923)
- *Madawaska Club, 1898–1973, Go Home Bay* (Toronto: The Club 1973)
- *The Rattler*, two small booklets dated August 15 and August 31, 1901, put out by the early Go Home Bay community

CHAPTER 1

– W. Arnot Craik, *Port Hope – Historical Sketches* (Port Hope, Ontario, 1901)
– *Mail and Empire*, Toronto, October 10, 1927. Remarks by Canon Cody, Chairman of the Board of Governors, University of Toronto
– *Port Hope Evening Guide*, December 5, 1979, extracted from the *Daily Guide*, January 20, 1909, obituary for Jane Anderson Galbraith

CHAPTER 2

– John Galbraith's personal diary, on the Fenian raid episode and the Foley survey
– John Galbraith's early professional life is based on his Application for the Chair of Civil Engineering in the School of Practical Science, Province of Ontario, 1878
– The story of the hemlock root comes from a personal letter to his mother, April 13, 1887
– Jacob Spelt, *Toronto*, Canadian Cities Series (Toronto: Collier Macmillan 1973)

Note: The Prince of Wales prize was offered annually after the Prince's visit to the university in 1860. It disappeared around 1880. The prize was an ornamental silver ink-stand worth $48. Candidates had to apply and state the subjects in which they would present themselves. The prize was awarded to the candidate with the highest aggregate number of marks in the subjects appointed for the examination for a B.A. degree, with honors in at least two departments and first-class standing in at least one. The candidate was also examined on books or subjects from previous years but not included in the final examination.

CHAPTERS 3 AND 8

Note: The original program at S.P.S. was for three years, with a diploma granted at the end. In 1891 a fourth year was added, with an additional certificate or diploma. In 1892 a student who completed the fourth year and wrote a thesis got the B.A.Sc. degree from the University for $10. Eventually the diplomas were phased out, and in 1909 the four-year program began leading to a B.A.Sc. degree only.

The civil engineer degree was a so-called professional degree awarded after the three-year diploma and at least three years of professional experience plus some examinations and a thesis. This was created in 1884. Three other professional degrees were added in 1896, in Mechanical, Electrical and Mining Engineering.

CHAPTER 4

- John Galbraith's article for the Quebec Geographical Society January 28, 1885, entitled "Canoe Trip from Lake Superior to Hudson Bay and Return via Lake Mistassini and the Saguenay River to Tadousac"
- John Galbraith's personal diary of his canoe trip of 1881
- Davis' Pain Killer: Sheila Kerr, *Early Prairie Remedies* Calgary: Glenbow Museum, 1981
- Peter C. Newman, *Company of Adventurers* (Penquin Books Canada 1985)

Note: In his diary and in his article for the Geographical Society, John Galbraith spells Tadoussac with one 's'. According to Pierre Georges Roy in *Les noms géographiques de la Province de Québec* (1906), the English wrote the name with one 's,' whereas the 'Canadians' wrote it with two, but pronounced it "Tad-oo-zac." I spell it with two, the way it is shown on the maps of today.

- p. 38 Metals were later found where John located the magnetic variation in the vicinity of Lake Mistassini.

CHAPTER 9

- John Galbraith's Address to Society of Civil Engineers, 1909, in *Applied Science*, Old Series Vol. 22, New Series, Vol. 11 No. 4, (Feb. 1909) pp 170–85
- John Galbraith's personal diary of Quebec Bridge Inquiry
- Report of the Royal Commission Quebec Bridge Inquiry (Ottawa: King's Printer 1908)